D1602877

REMEMBERING
THE FUTURE

THE CHARLES ELIOT NORTON LECTURES

REMEMBERING THE FUTURE

Luciano Berio

HARVARD UNIVERSITY PRESS

Cambridge, Massachusetts ▐ London, England   2006

Library of Congress Cataloging-in-Publication Data
Berio, Luciano, 1925-
Remembering the future / Luciano Berio.
p. cm.—(The Charles Eliot Norton lectures)
Contents: Formations—Translating music—Forgetting music—
O alter Duft—Seeing music—Poetics of analysis.
ISBN 0-674-02154-1 (alk. paper)
1. Music—History and criticism.
2. Composers. I. Title. II. Series.

ML60.B4685 2006
780—dc22   2005056706

PREFACE

Talia Pecker Berio

Luciano Berio delivered the Charles Eliot Norton lectures at Harvard University during the academic year 1993–94. Each lecture was introduced and concluded by the performance of one of Berio's *Sequenze*—a series of fourteen compositions for solo instruments that cover the entire arc of his career. Berio conceived of their presence not as "illustrations" of the lectures, but rather as "musical quotation marks intended to protect the audience from the inevitable incompleteness and factiousness of any discourse on music made by a musician."

Two close friends and longtime collaborators preceded Berio in this prestigious series of lectures. Umberto Eco read his *Six Walks in the Fictional Woods* during the spring semester of 1993; the title of his book and its opening pages pay homage to Italo Calvino, who was about to depart for Cambridge to deliver his *Six Memos for the Next Millennium* when he suddenly passed away in September 1985. The affinity of spirit and the experiences shared with both authors can be traced within and between the lines in various passages of Berio's own lectures. It is no coincidence, then, that he derived their title from *Un re in ascolto*—one of his three music-theater works with texts by Calvino. "Remembering the future" is hardly a literal translation of the more ambiguous original "*ricordo al futuro*"—the closing words pronounced by Prospero, the key figure of *Un re in ascolto,* who takes his leave from life questioning voice and silence, turning memory back and forth, from and toward the future:

> *la memoria custodisce il silenzio*
> *ricordo del futuro la promessa*
> *quale promessa? questa che ora arrivi*
> *a sfiorare col lembo della voce*
> *e ti sfugge come il vento accarezza*
> *il buio nella voce il ricordo*
> *in penombra un ricordo al futuro.*

> Memory stands guard over silence
> recollection of the future the promise
> which promise? this one that now you may
> barely touch with the voice's extremity
> and that slips from your mind as the wind caresses
> the darkness in the voice the memory
> in the shadows a memory for the future.

> <small>(TRANSLATION BY DAVID OSMOND-SMITH)</small>

This interplay of past and present, of remembering and forgetting, is ever present in the following pages, but it is always underpinned by an unshakable faith in the future, and in the power of music to cross distances, to give voice and shape to that interplay and faith.

The content and structure of these lectures were defined and sketched out over a long period following the appointment as Norton lecturer, which was formalized at the beginning of 1992. By the time we settled in Cambridge in the fall of 1993, the first two lectures were substantially written out, but work on them, as on each of the other four lectures, proceeded until the very time of their delivery, and sometimes well afterward. All of them were written in Italian, translated into English by Anthony Oldcorn, and then further elaborated by Berio himself.

In the years following our residence at Harvard, Berio was engaged in the composition of two major works of music theater, *Outis* (1996) and *Cronaca del Luogo* (1999), and a considerable number of instrumental works such as *Ekphrasis* for orchestra; *Alternatim* for viola, clarinet, and orchestra; *Solo* for trombone and orchestra; *Kol od* (*Chemins VI* for trumpet and chamber orchestra); *Récit* (*Chemins VII* for alto saxophone and orchestra); *Sonata* for piano; the last three *Sequenze* (XII for bassoon, XIII for accordion, XIV for cello), as well as *Altra voce* (for alto flute, mezzo-soprano, and live electronics), and the new Finale for Puccini's *Turandot*. He completed his last work, *Stanze* for baritone, three male choirs, and orchestra, a few weeks before he left us on May 27, 2003.

Thus the final revision of the Norton Lectures was constantly delayed, yet work on them was never entirely abandoned. Periodically, between one composition and another, Berio would go back to them, introducing minor changes, pointing out passages in need of major revision, taking notes for further developments. This "work in progress" (an important concept in Berio's poetics, which recurs frequently in the following pages, especially in the fourth lecture, "O alter Duft") involved both the Italian and English texts. As a result there were often multiple versions of each lecture, none of which, at the moment of the author's death, could be declared as "definite"; nor was it always possible to establish the chronological order of the variants.

Confronted with such a complex source situation, I decided to follow the texts of the lectures as they were read at Harvard, correcting and integrating them only in those places where the variant readings were either objectively clearer or undoubtedly approved by the author. I felt that this approach conveyed more coherence to the text (in contrast to a more orthodox philological editing method), and I was inspired as well by Robert Schumann's youthful and romantic idea that "the first conception of a work is always the best and most natural."

Any attempt to acknowledge on behalf of my husband the people who accompanied him in the process of writing and revising the lectures would necessarily be incomplete. David Osmond-Smith, Luciana Galliano, and Anthony Oldcorn would undoubtedly have been among them. I can personally testify to the constant and inspiring exchanges he had with Reinhold Brinkmann, the late David Lewin, and Christoph Wolff, who, along with Dorothea, June, and Barbara, gave warmth to our season in Cambridge with their priceless friendship. Mark Kagan and Nancy Shiffman helped in every possible way to make our life and work, as well as the meetings and performances at Sanders Theatre, smooth and enjoyable. Peg Fulton of Harvard University Press patiently accompanied the long genesis of *Remembering the Future* from the day of Berio's appointment to the Norton Chair down to the last detail of this edition.

My personal thanks go to Reinhold Brinkmann, who provided me with the only intact printed copy that has survived of the full set of six lectures: at the end of each lecture, Luciano would ritually hand him a copy of the text that he had just read out. In a different time this would have been the "engraver's copy"; I have tried to conduct my editing accordingly, with the economy and respect that was common before the computer era, and was lucky to have Mary Ellen Geer as an exceptionally sensitive editor. Marina Berio had read and commented upon her father's lectures at the time of their delivery; she was at my side last summer to give a loving and knowing hand in the revision of the text. I would like—and feel that Luciano would have approved—to dedicate this book to her, to Cristina, Stefano, Daniel, and Jonathan Berio.

RADICONDOLI (SIENA), OCTOBER 2005

CONTENTS

REMEMBERING
THE FUTURE

FORMATIONS

The honor of delivering the Norton Lectures coincides with my desire to express my doubts about the possibility of offering today a unified vision of musical thought and practice, and of mapping out a homogeneous and linear view of recent musical developments. I am not even sure that we can find a guiding thread through the intricate musical maze of the last few decades, nor do I intend to attempt a taxonomy, or seek to define the innumerable ways of coming to grips with the music we carry with us.

Of course, I am not inviting you to abandon words and take refuge in purely sensory experiences—nor to play games with music in some hermeneutic "hall of mirrors." But I would like to suggest to you some points of reference that I have found useful in my work, and in my reflections on that strange, fascinating Babel of musical behaviors that surrounds us.

I like to remember the last words that Italo Calvino wrote for the closing of my music-theater work *Un Re in Ascolto,* when the protagonist departs from life, saying: "a recollection of the future." This, I feel, sums up my concerns in these lectures. I will not concern myself here with music as an emotional and reassuring commodity for the listener, nor with music as a procedural and reassuring commodity for the composer. It is my intention to share with you some musical experiences that invite us to revise or suspend our relation with the past, and to rediscover it as part of a future trajectory.

Such an exercise in revision may lead us into a *selva oscura*—Dante's "dark forest." But unlike Dante, we will have to sacrifice paths, voluntarily lost and found, and behave like Brechtian actors with their famous *Verfremdung:* we will have to step outside ourselves, observe and question what we do. We need to question the very idea of a musical reality that can be defined or translated by words, and therefore the idea of a linear relationship between the empirical and conceptual dimensions of music. We also need to challenge the idea that musical experience could be compared to a huge, protective building, designed by history and constructed over several millennia by countless men (and now, finally, also by women). Not that we could ever get to see a floor plan, a cross-section, or a profile of this immense metaphorical building. We might wander through a few rooms, trying to grasp the content and function of each of them (the Ars nova room, the Baroque room, the Schubert, Mahler, and Stravinsky rooms, the Viennese, the Darmstadt, the "set theory" rooms—and, why not, the minimalist and the post-modern rooms), but in doing so we would be conditioned by what we had already heard and known; we would then reinterpret each experience, modify its perspective, and therefore also the building's global history. The history of such modifications is the history of our actions and ideas, which sometimes seem to run ahead of the arrival of the actual work that will embody them. If that were not so, our metaphorical building would become a homogeneous and unanimous space, deterministically subject to so-called historical necessities, and therefore musically useless.

At the same time, however, we are aware that we are only able to know and to explain those musical experiences that have already taken place, those virtualities that have been fully realized. The history of music, unlike the history of science, is never made of intents but of achievements. It is not made of potential forms waiting to be shaped but, rather, of Texts (with a capital "T" and with the largest possible musical connotations). It is made of Texts waiting to be interpreted—conceptually, emotionally, and practically.

In music, as in literature, it may be plausible to conceive a reciprocal shifting of focus between the text's supremacy over the reader and the primacy of the reader becoming his or her own text. As Harold Bloom remarked, "you are, or you become what you read" and "that which you are, that only can you read."

The implications of these statements are endless. When applied to music they have to take into account performance, so that the question of supremacy becomes overly complicated: to perform and interpret a musical text is obviously not the same thing as to read and interpret a literary one. Perhaps the difficulties composers encounter when they talk about texts arise from their feeling that they themselves are a musical Text, that they live inside a text and therefore are lacking the detachment necessary to explore, with some objectivity, the nature of the relation they entertain with themselves as text. It is not an accident that the most rewarding commentaries written by composers are on other composers, and that composer-writers—such as Schumann and Debussy—were "hiding" behind a pseudonym. The same may be true today, even without pseudonyms, provided that the main concern of the composer who comments on the work of another composer is other than to prove that his analysis "works" and that it is immune from preconditionings.

I tend to admire "analytical listening" and the so-called "analytical performers," but I also believe that a delicate balance must be maintained, at whatever cost, between recognition of conventions, stylistic references, expectations, and, on the other hand, the concrete experience of giving a new life to an object of knowledge. In fact, performers, listeners, and indeed composers undergo a sort of alchemical transformation in which recognition, knowledge, and conceptual associations— all fruits of their relationship with Texts—are spontaneously transformed into a live entity, a "being" which transcends and sublimates technical realities. An "intertextual" conditioning can become so imposing that the measure in which the speakers are themselves spoken may be the same that would deprive the speaker of the courage to speak.

When James Joyce said that his *Ulysses* would keep scholars busy for at least a hundred years, he was of course displaying his Mephistophelian nature. He knew that scholars would not be able to resist the temptation to identify references and allusions, once they knew they were there. But he also knew that living with the "half-recognized" and with deceptive identities was an important dimension of *Ulysses*—as it is of any form of poetry.

It is the pinning down per se—as if to prove the permanent legitimacy of a detail—that deprives the narrative of its dynamic and still unknown potentials. It may happen in music, too, that the capacity to identify, to remember, and to hold together a network of references can become poisonous unless it is balanced by a willingness to forget and to communicate even without addressees and without a conscious relation to specific listening codes. We know it in depth when we perform or create music; when we raise, even unawares, the eternal question of our relationship with the text and the text's relationship with us: a question that music can address only through the acceptance of a silent text.

The attempt to establish a dialectic between music's practical and conceptual dimensions goes back a long way and has sometimes assumed a radical epistemological importance. For this reason I propose that we pay a fleeting, non-archaeological visit to the Roman philosopher Severinus Boethius, who rose to fame in the early sixth century A.D. He was also a musical theorist. For him music was a silent text; it was indeed one of the chief tools of philosophical speculation; it was governed by numbers, and was therefore "harmonic." The laws of the universe were, for Boethius as for Pythagoras before him, laws of an essentially musical nature. Deriving the concept of music from the Greeks and proposing it to his contemporaries (and to the entire Middle Ages), Boethius conceived music above all as a means of knowledge. His evaluation of beauty in its relation to art and to music is secondary. His vision stems from Stoicism, a philosophy according to which beauty is a question of appearances and hence has a purely formal value. Although his speculations on music induced him to praise Pythagoras for having tackled the subject without making any reference to the faculty of hearing, Boethius claimed that the surest path to the human soul passed through the ear. Of this he had no doubt. Music, he wrote, affects human behavior, and so it is essential to be aware of its constituent parts and of its ethical value. This Neoplatonic view of the musical ethos reflects the idea of music as part of the medieval *quadrivium,* together with arithmetic, geometry, and astronomy—the higher division of the seven liberal arts (the others being grammar, rhetoric, and logic: the *trivium*).

In his *De Institutione Musica* Boethius discusses the Pythagorean theory of proportions and celebrates music as a tool of the universal logic embedded in everything: when it reflects the harmony of the universe it is *musica mundana;* when it expresses the interior harmony of the soul it becomes *musica humana;* when it is practical and emerges in the voice and in musical instruments it is *musica instrumentalis.* According to Boethius music is, above all, pure knowledge, whereas poetry, conceived to be recited or sung, is indeed an "art of sound," and we may therefore leave it to poets to compose songs, to play them and sing them.

How then shall we approach Boethius's teaching? As a kind of philosophical manifesto of abstract musical functions, or as a very distant ancestor of our segmented musical world?

I am raising these questions to remind you that the need to conduct conceptual speculations parallel and perhaps prior to concrete musical experience has very deep and long-standing roots. Boethius's theoretical proposal did not attempt to formalize experiences that had already taken place or a practice under way, but instead he appropriated *in advance* the experience of sound, while conditioning its very formation and development.

A persistent analysis of the links between theory and practice and the tendency to theorize and formalize musical behavior is an obvious, universal aspect of our culture. It underlies the notion of music as Text, as a document of an investment and of an encounter of ideas and experiences. But these days we have no permanent conceptual tools, no theory of proportions, of the affects *(die Affektenlehre)* of harmonic functions, not even of total serialization. We don't have *trivium* or *quadrivium,* and we don't live in a homogeneous musical society. Nor do we have a *lingua franca* that would allow us a free and peaceful passage from one musical domain to another.

What we do have at our disposal, instead, is an immense library of musical knowledge, which attracts or intimidates us, inviting us to suspend or to confound our chronologies. For over a century composers have been taking metaphorical trips to the library, to take stock of its endless shelves. I'm thinking for example of Brahms and Mahler, or of the 1920s, when the very different neoclassicisms of Stravinsky and Schoenberg, both tireless and motivated visitors to an immense "music reading-room," might be seen as the two faces of the same attempt at "exorcising" the overwhelming presence of the library itself—a library that is unable to offer coherence, but can receive it from the right visitors. Today that library has become boundless. Rather like Borges' "Library of Babel," it spreads out in all directions; it has no *before* nor *after,* no place for storing memories. It is always open, totally present, but awaiting interpretation.

I think that the search for a "universal" answer to the questions raised by musical experience will never be completely fulfilled; but we know that a question raised is often more significant than the answer received. Only a reckless spirit, today, would try to give a total explanation of music, but anyone who would never pose the problem is even more reckless. I don't believe that thought is a form of silent speech: we can think and conceptualize music without referring to speech. Music evades verbal discourse and tends to spill over the edges of any analytical container. This fact, and the dialectical nature of the relationship between the idea of practice and the practice of the idea, have brought music analysis into the domain of signs. But the question is, what can music analysis mean when it recurs to semiology (a semiology based mainly on linguistics) in order to investigate the relation between concept and perception— two dimensions which are in constant adjustment, and whose reciprocal "betrayal" is at the root of musical experience?

My view of linguistic units may appear somewhat simplistic, but it seems to me that the linguistic sign is not translatable into musical terms. Let's look at the binary, pragmatic elements of language: signifier and signified, *signans* and *signatum,* deep level and surface level, *langue* and *parole,* and also the binary use of distinctive features: the relationship between them, when transposed into music, turns out to be *significantly* undefinable. The binary elements themselves are not readily identifiable even in the highly structured and codified classical forms which were the most "linguistic" in music history (like the sonatas of Haydn and Mozart). The semiological misunderstanding stems from the fact that linguistic categories are applied to a musical texture whose morphological and syntactical elements cannot be separated. Furthermore, all the elements of language—grammar, syntax, morphology, lexical content, and so on—have to work together in a way established by culture, whereas a similar solidarity among musical elements has to be constantly reconsidered. It is no coincidence that Gestalt theory developed on the basis of what you see, rather than what you hear. In language, a word implies and excludes many different things, said and unsaid, and the name of a thing is not the thing itself. Whereas the musical "word," the musical utterance, is always *the thing itself.*

A melody by Schubert or a musical configuration by Schoenberg are not the pieces of a musical chessboard; they carry within themselves the experience of other melodies and other configurations, and their transformations are inscribed, so to speak, in their genetic code. This self-sufficiency gives musical experience an enormous associative and semantic openness, of such an uncoded nature that a semiologist may be able to come to grips only with interpretive codes implied in listening and (more important) in re-listening, rather than with creative and structuring processes. And that is why an algorithm that describes the significative processes of music is still wishful thinking. Unlike language, music cannot become "meta-music," and unless you make a very trivial use of it, musical metaphors and metonymies simply do not exist. Nor can it be deconstructed: in fact deconstructivist foxes don't seem to be tempted by eating musical grapes—perhaps they think they are still sour.

It has been said that each language is able to reflect on itself, to think about itself. Music too is able to do so, despite the impossibility of translating it into terms of language. But the point is that every musical work is a set of partial systems that interact among themselves, not merely because they are active at the same time, but because they establish a sort of organic and unstable reciprocity. Without that instability we enter a rather fascinating and uncomfortable musical space—we like to think about it but we don't have to listen to it—as is the case with works like Schoenberg's Wind Quintet or Boulez's First Book of *Structures* for two pianos.

We like to think that music performs itself before it ever comes to performance, not only because a composer can play it out silently in his or her mind, but also because all of its meaningful layers exhibit conceptually both their autonomy and their reciprocal interactions.

Let's imagine a pitch-cell, for instance, or a pitch-sequence that generates melodies, figures, phrases, and harmonic processes. A rhythmic configuration shapes those melodies and generates patterns, time glissandos, and discontinuous or even statistical distributions of those same melodies and figures. Dynamic layers, instrumental colors and techniques, can nullify or enhance the individual characters of each process, the nature of their evolution, and the degree of their independence. At times, that independence can become indifference and the musical parameters can follow their own life, their own autonomous time of evolution, like some of the characters from Robert Musil's narrative.

To think out music entails separating those processes but, also, cultivating an inner, implicit dialogue among them, a polyphony made of varying degrees of interaction which, on occasion, can explode and absorb everything in a dazzling, synthetic gesture. Simple, neutral, and periodic pitch and time relations, situated in a homogeneous timbric and dynamic texture, will fuse into transparent events, colored by the given harmonic relations. Complex and discontinuous intervallic and rhythmic relations, distributed among very diversified instrumental forces, will fuse into a noise. These explosions, these all-embracing gestures, are analogous to the speeding up of a visual sequence in a film, where specific details will be transformed and blend into lines of movement.

Extreme situations, from the simple to the very complex, will entail different and often contradictory ways of listening, from the most analytical to the most global, from the most active to the most passive. This instability, this mobility of perspectives, must be carefully composed as part of a meaningful musical architecture, and occasionally can stretch to the point of opening itself to outside visitors, to strangers, to happenings, to musical figures coherently loaded with associations. I have explored that possibility myself in works like *Visage* or in the fifth part of my *Sinfonia*.

A musically significant work is always made of interacting meaningful layers that are at once the agents and the materials of its existence. They are the actor, the director, and the script all in one—or, rather, they are like the lake of an Indian tale, which sets out in search of its own source. So what is the musical Text? Is it the water itself, or the urge to seek out the source, the wellspring?

It has been said that music changes because its materials change. While it is true that the advent of iron and glass brought about a change in architecture, it is also true that architectural thought had already changed and was thus prepared to perceive how iron and glass might be used. The old sound-generators in the electronic music studios of the 1950s did not change the essence of music. Musical thinking had already changed the moment musicians began to consider the possibility of a meaningful interaction between additive and subtractive criteria, looking, for instance, for a structural continuity between timbre and harmony. Those archaic packets of sinusoidal waves, or those variable bands of filtered white noise, were mostly the end-result of the extreme concentration of intervallic functions in the poetic world of Anton Webern: the three notes of his generative cells (*multum in parvo,* in a true Goethian perspective) that are at once different and always the same.

We have come a long way in the studios of electronic music since those distant post-Webernian beginnings. The criteria of sound-assembling that often steered research in those days (criteria which have continued to influence the beginnings of computer-assisted music) had widened the gap between theory and practice, between a thought and its realization that was assigned to a magnetic or digital memory. This had an influence also on the notation of instrumental music, at least in those cases where the conception of a work prompted doubts as to whether a score should provide graphic prescriptions for its performance, or descriptions of the sound result, or, simply and fatalistically, should be a form of prognostication, a way of guessing.

An ultimate sign of the gap between thought and acoustic end-result came about when the musical score became an aesthetic object to be admired only visually—the eye becoming a substitute for the ear, supposedly triggering undecipherable musical sensations in the viewer. The extreme was reached, I suppose, when a pianist was instructed to play strings of dots, blotches of ink, or the graph of someone's heartbeat. But I don't wish to make fun of those experiences. Some were very amusing and ironic; viewed as a whole, they had their roots both in the *angst* over communication and in the circuit of marketable art objects.

Turning the score into a visual object may allow associations to proliferate. It may evoke the "beauty" of Bach's manuscripts, or the "ugliness" of Beethoven's sketches; but that "beauty" and that "ugliness" have nothing to do with musical processes and functions: they are mere aestheticized gestures that, in their detachment from any form of musical thought and from its realization in sound, become a para-musical merchandise, as superficial and self-promoting as those "new sounds" that often end up as *jingles,* advertising a singular absence of musical thought.

Nevertheless, there is also something attractive in the unwillingness to bridge the gap between musical gesture and acoustic result. I am thinking of that sacrificial and somehow clownish impulse that seeks to defy an object in its original function: a piano becomes a gamelan or the workshop of a happily mindless ironsmith; the concert hall is filled with the amplified sounds of whales or the noises of intergalactic magnetic storms . . . It is possible to see in this rejection of the "artistic" a link with the studiedly "careless" art of Marcel Duchamp (think of his ready-mades, of his *Mona Lisa* with a moustache and a "hot bottom," of his urinal, that is, his *Fountain*)—as exemplary as that of John Cage, to whom I dedicate these thoughts.

The removal of behavior from musical functions and from cultural conditionings, and the stubborn and somehow mystical defense of a persistent gap between musical thought and acoustic materialization, have produced not only ironic and paroxystic social gestures, but also some eminently useful consequences. It has often had a liberating effect (early Cage is a telling example), opening up a space, perhaps more virtual than real, for non-applied musical research, a research that was not tied to specific functions and results, nor to explicitly musical regulatory principles.

All of this occurred a long time ago, in the "roaring fifties," when I personally was busy looking for harmonic coherence between diverse materials, in a musical context made of sounds and not only of notes. Without that freedom of thought and action, my musical research into the human voice would probably have developed in different ways and over a different span of time. During those years I was particularly involved in developing different degrees and modes of continuity between the human voice, instruments, and a poetic text, or between vocal sound-families and interrelated electronic sounds. *Circles,* based on three poems by e. e. cummings, and *Visage,* for voice and electronic sounds, were the result of this development.

That liberating effect also manifested itself in procedural and mainly arithmetical speculation into the separation and isolation of acoustic-musical parameters. This was a fundamental and cathartic experience which had its roots, again, in Schoenberg's and Webern's thinking, and was tied to visions of organic musical development. Most of Webern's works, especially after the String Trio op. 20, are no longer explicitly thematic, yet they deal with thematic virtualities which are at the same time the result and the generators of thematic processes. They could generate themes, but they stop just short of doing so, also because they undergo a constant process of variation. That hidden, thematic virtuality deepens and enriches our perspective of Webern's music, enhancing the notion of form, material, and musical matter as relative concepts.

In one of his seminal writings on Webern, Pierre Boulez reminds us of Webern's own assertion that "the choice of tone-rows is no more innocent than it is arbitrary." Webern justifies his choice with the wealth of structural relations that it contains—relations that foster a form of development that cannot be termed "thematic" because it always remains a kernel. The notion of kernel became increasingly important to Webern toward the end of his life, when he referred frequently to Goethe's *Metamorphosis of Plants:* "The stem is already contained in the root, the leaf in the stem, and the flower in turn in the leaf: it is all a variation of the same idea." Although Goethe's statement is hardly a scientific revelation, the image it conveys is of fundamental importance in structural and poetic terms, that is, in terms of the formation of musical meanings.

Carl Dahlhaus pointed out a similar idea regarding the relationship between material and matter: "The brick is the form of the piece of clay, the house is the form of the bricks, the village is the form of the house." I would like to bring this quotation closer to my own point of view, inverting the order of the images to fit a subtractive rather than additive perspective: "The village is the form of the house, the house is the form of the brick, the brick is the form of the piece of clay." And here, again, is the same lake which sets out in search of its sources while dialoguing with them. In other words, the elaboration of the cell with additive criteria can be temporarily suspended, and the path that leads to musical sense may move in an opposite direction, calling upon subtractive criteria to a heterogeneous, even chaotic whole of acoustical data. Like the sculptor who extracts the sculpture, *a forza di levare* (as Michelangelo said), from the block of marble. Such criteria may lead to the discovery of a specific figure: the generating cell.

Post-Webernian serialists extracted from Webern's poetics those elements that would give concrete and conceptual drive to the break with the past. These elements were the autonomy and the equivalence of musical parameters often submitted to indifferent permutational procedures—so indifferent that music could go on forever. It could not end; it could only stop. Grounded in permutational and equalizing criteria, and essentially lacking virtual or hidden dimensions, it was soon neutralized by the objective impossibility of generating significantly evolving structures. The end of the "separatist" movement was brought about, oedipally, by the very serial conceptions and procedures that had generated it—but without complexes. The excess of estranged formal order generated disorder—just as the hyper-thematization of Webern's music obliterated themes as such.

During the fifties music went through a period of fixation on homogeneity, which tended to prevent each parameter from assuming a real and expressive autonomy of development as part of a polyphony of musical functions. Schoenberg's *Farben,* from op. 16, the ellipses and false symmetries of Debussy's *La Mer* and *Jeux,* the "timbre-chords" of Webern's Second Cantata, op. 31, and Stravinsky's fleeting meditations on history, from *Le Chant du Rossignol* to *Agon,* had not yet found attentive ears. At one stage, the conflicting obsession with neutrality and separation led to an attempt to separate out the "parameters" of creativity itself—in other words, to separate the lake from its source. Attempts were made to distinguish various types of creativity on the basis of their supposed contents, proposing, for instance, an opposition between *style* and *expression,* where the notion of *style* was ideologically labeled as a perverted product of the cultural market while, symmetrically, the idea of *expression* was positively embedded in the rigorous and self-depriving anger of the avant-gardes.

The urge to split and divide, which has pervaded the musical world for the last few decades, has also postulated an opposition between the empirical musician (who has no need for "synthesis," and is subject to circumstances) and the systematic musician (who starts with a preconceived idea, and follows an all-embracing strategy)—in other words, an opposition between the composer as *bricoleur* and the composer as scientist. But creation is simply not available to this unproductive dichotomy: the scientific or systematic musician and the empirical musician have always coexisted, they must coexist, complementing each other in the same person. A deductive vision has to be able to interact with an inductive vision. Likewise, an additive "philosophy" of musical creation has to interrelate with a subtractive "philosophy." Or again, the structural elements of a musical process have to enter into relation with the concrete, acoustical dimensions of its articulation: with the voices that sing it, and the instruments that play it.

In a significant and coherent musical itinerary, as visionary and disruptive as you please, the separation between the global and individual, and between the real and virtual dimensions is inevitably projected into a plurality of orbits that transform their meaning. They become formations of sense that cannot be reduced to their functioning.

An essential factor of modernity has always been its ability to modify perspectives, to cancel or multiply the vanishing points, the "tonics" that indicate the "right" path, and to construct something from the remains of what has been transformed, sublimated, and even destroyed. It could be said that the realm of tonal music, too, launches its themes and all its constituent parts into orbit, modifying their sense and perspective. But these constituents—though possessing a great number of variables—were always part of a more or less permanent and recognizable physiognomy, always tied to general behavioral criteria: like the changes of expression that are an integral part of the human face. The degree of awareness and familiarity of the constituent "physiognomic" features and of the changes of expression was conditioned by the experience of historically activated and accepted relationships between the structural elements and the peripheral elements, between implicit functions and explicit features, and between the different degrees of transformation of the whole. Tonal music was above all a vast and widely shared cultural experience that involved its participants, musicians and listeners alike, in a huge variety of musical relationships. For the musicians the knowledge of music was similar to the knowledge of nature. The composer produced music in a theoretical bedrock mostly taken for granted. Theory itself was primarily an account of experience. As with tonal grammar and syntax, forms (such as the fugue, and above all the sonata form) were likewise analyzed and formalized *post factum,* after the experience.

Today, theoretical outlooks tend to emerge before practice, with consequences that are perhaps less enduring than those experienced by Boethius, though no less significant. A theoretical manifesto has indeed become a declaration of poetics. Schoenberg was the first, of course, to carry out this idea of modernity. The experience of twelve-tone theory, which had both its heroes and its victims (especially among those who approached it as a linguistic norm), is in fact the attempt to formalize Schoenberg's own poetics—one of the most generous, complex, and dramatic of our history.

In the process of rebuilding and revising the past with our recollection of the future, we cannot invent a new, utopian musical language, nor can we invent its instruments. Yet we contribute continuously to their evolution.

Once, experience of musical instruments preceded any theoretical awareness of creativity. Instruments were the keys that allowed one to enter the edifice of musical speculation. Until Wagner all composers, with the exception of some opera composers, were virtuoso performers in their own right. With Mahler, Debussy, and the Viennese School there was a conspicuous shifting away from that individual virtuosity, which had previously been synonymous with musical knowledge and professional excellence. Meanwhile, the orchestra became the "collective" instrument of the composer. The "maestro di cappella," the Kapellmeister at the harpsichord, became the conductor of a symphony orchestra, that is, the coordinator of increasingly differentiated stylistic and technical concerns. Musical creativity became gradually divorced from its specific tools, with a growing detachment from those marvelous acoustic machines.

Musical instruments are tools useful to man, but they are tools that lack objectivity: they produce sounds that are anything but neutral, which acquire meaning by testing meaning itself with the reality of facts. They are the concrete depositories of historical continuity and, like all working tools and buildings, they have a memory. They carry with them traces of the musical and social changes and of the conceptual framework within which they were developed and transformed. They talk music and—not without conflicts—they let themselves be talked by it. The sounds produced by keys, strings, wood, and metal are in turn all tools of knowledge, and contribute to the making of the idea itself. *Verbum caro factum est* (the word became flesh), with sweat and technique.

Musical instruments act and think with us and, at times, in our "absentminded" moments, they even think *for* us. For the composer-performer of the Baroque, Classical, and Romantic periods, improvisation was a form of instantaneous, real-time composing (which has parallels, albeit through different codes, with jazz improvisation). Nowadays this form of *extempore* composition is no longer possible because the numerous stratifications of musical thought, together with compositional strategies always "in progress" between idea and realization, do not allow the composer to escape the conscious presence and definition of a musical text which in any case (even outside the frame of improvisation) cannot be totally handled in real time with carefree spontaneity.

As depository of tradition and technique, the musical instrument can become either a weapon against easygoing amnesias or a fetish, a sort of "still life," a motionless object, a nostalgic reminder of a hypothetical paradise lost. Even if locked away, unplayed, in a room, the image of a musical instrument—a powerful Steinway or a priceless Stradivarius—can take a symbolic absolute value, substituting for music itself. This fetish became, among other things, the target of John Cage's irony and provocative suggestions.

Instruments take a long time to transform themselves, and they tend to lag behind the evolution of musical thought. The violin, for instance, virtually unaltered, has been inhabited by the history of music of the last four hundred years. It has an imposing legacy, and for this reason, whichever way it is played, it expresses that history and heritage—even if you tune it completely differently, or interface it with a MIDI system.

The same thing may be said for nearly all the musical instruments we know. The six strings of the guitar, for instance, are tuned in a very idiomatic way which is largely responsible for the harmonic colors of many orchestral "postcards" from sunny Spain, but also for other musical exploits of a less picturesque but far more subtle nature (as in Ravel's "Spanish music" or in several of Debussy's piano accompaniments). To overlook or to ignore this idiolectic aspect of the musical instrument, and the host of technical details and performance styles associated with it, may be an interesting exercise from an ascetic point of view, but is undeniably impoverishing. It is indicative of a difficulty in matching ideas and theoretical reflections with the reality of the musical instrument (or voice) which, for the history it embodies and for the ways and techniques through which it inhabits history, is already expressive in itself. As always, it is not musical thinking which has to submit itself to the instrument; rather, it is thought itself that must become a conscious container for the instrument and its physical legacy.

The history of music has always been marked by new ways

of engaging with instruments and with the human voice. Occasionally a new kind of dialogue has been established. Consider the instrumental inventions that Monteverdi generated from his ideas on *stile rappresentativo.* Consider Bach's solo violin partitas, which run the entire gamut of violin techniques—past, present, and future. Or the piano music of Beethoven, in which the instrument is transformed into a musical volcano (I am thinking of the "Waldstein" Sonata, of op. 106, op. 111, and the Diabelli Variations). Later on, the keyboard-dialogue becomes tougher but still extremely constructive. I am thinking of Bartók, Stravinsky, Messiaen, Stockhausen, Boulez, Carter, Ligeti, and some of my own piano works. Now and then the instrumental debate has generated a sort of sly indifference, or has escalated to a real clash, to an outright rebellion, in which the instrument becomes, as we have seen, a fetish to be desecrated.

We certainly have within us a constant need to transcend instruments, but we also know that we cannot go beyond them without eventually coming back, and setting up a dialogue with them. We can never contribute to their evolution if we treat them as mere sound generators and ignore their history. If we do that, we are just sticking our heads in the sand. Now, ostriches have never contributed significant forms of evolution, nor have they ever considered the problem of creating a dialogue (however metaphorical) between "heaven" (the idea) and earth, between the "soul" and the body (the instrument)—or, if you think that the jump is worth the effort (always metaphorical, of course), between *musica mundana, musica humana,* and *musica instrumentalis.* Any form of creativity that is untouched by the desire to bridge this persistent and significant gap is condemned to silence.

Now, let me conclude this introductory journey from Boethius to the guitar with one particular point. I am deeply fascinated by musical ideas which manage to develop a polyphony of different formations of meaning—ideas that do not reject the possibility of dealing with specific and concrete instrumental gestures which then set up a whole range of distant echoes and memories, allowing us to establish a dialogue of specific presences and absences: a musical space inhabited by the significant presence of absences and by the echo of absent presences.

However, there is a new factor that makes this a difficult and yet appealing enterprise: it is the sheer wealth of thought and the enormous, pluralistic diversity of musical behaviors surrounding us. This reality obliges us to question everything: even the most concrete implications of our intellectual tools.

Since, fortunately, we don't live with a totalizing (or should I say a "tonalizing") view of music, we can permit ourselves to explore and bring together the various strata, the various formations of meaning in our musical journey. In doing so we should not forget that heterogeneity and pluralism have to translate themselves into processes and ideas, not into forms and manners—forms are often misleading, as they can be perceived independently of their meaning.

It is precisely because of this multiplicity of relationships— often conflicting, but even more often complementary in a constructive way—that we sometimes find ourselves faced with vast, uncharted domains, halfway between heaven and earth, between the *musica mundana* and the *musica instrumentalis*. And then we are assailed by doubt as to whether music can actually venture further into the domains that it has itself created, or link up these far-flung points, and we suddenly wonder if music alone is enough, whether it will succeed. But that is precisely when we become acutely aware that music, though self-significant, is never alone; that its potential problems—if they are such—come from somewhere else; and that we must continue to question it relentlessly in all of its aspects, in all the folds of its tireless body and of its endlessly generous soul.

2

TRANSLATING MUSIC

Music is translated, apparently, only when a specific need aris-
es and we are compelled to go from the actual musical experience to its verbal description, from the sound of one instrument to another, or from the silent reading of a musical text
to its performance. In reality this need is so pervasive and permanent that we are tempted to say that the history of music is
indeed a history of translations. But perhaps all of our history,
the entire development of our culture, is a history of translations. Our culture has to possess everything, therefore it translates everything: languages of all kinds, things, concepts, facts,
emotions, money, the past and the future, and, of course,
music.

Translation implies interpretation. The seventy sages of
Alexandria who translated the Bible into Greek "invented"
hermeneutics. We are well aware of the implication of Luther's
translation of the Bible into the German language, the French
translation of the American Bill of Rights, the cultural and
spiritual flux linking Greek to Latin, and Latin to the "vul-
gar" romance tongues in Dante's time. In all of these occasions

translation was, in fact, a hermeneutic practice, an interpretation of a text, and the acquisitions were by no means one-way, from a language of departure to a language of arrival. The same multidirectional interaction occurs today, in the borrowings that take place between hegemonic languages (like English, for example) and national languages, between standard national languages and local dialects, between oral and written traditions.

Can observations on literary translation be applied, by analogy, to translation in music, in other words to transcription? Definitely yes, even if there is an obvious difference between a written text available to all to read, interpret, and translate and a score to be performed. Language is an instrument of common and practical verbal communication, but it can also be literature, prose and poetry. Music is always "literature," and its transcriptions, which often imply a vast and complex network of interactions, will never present their author with the dilemma that the translator of poetry must often face: whether to be more faithful to the meaning or to the wording of a poem, that is, whether to betray one dimension for the sake of the other.

Literature itself can be a transcription of a long-standing tradition of oral narrative techniques. It has been argued that Homer's *Iliad* and *Odyssey* are in reality collective works that were handed down, elaborated, and gradually crystallized over a period of about five centuries. The tales and myths became fused in poetic format, and their written transcription often reveals the use of specific narrative devices, such as repetition, frequent reminders of the heroes' fame and accomplishments, phrases that fit in neatly with the hexameters, and so forth. Ulysses narrates his adventures, adapting them to suit the expectations and conventions of those to whom he speaks. Was he a liar? If the *Odyssey* were not the transcription of oral sources, of rhetoric conventions and narrative techniques, Ulysses would perhaps not have come down to us as such an astute hero.

Art music too can rely on transcriptions of oral traditions; we all know this and, having learned a lot from Béla Bartók, I am myself particularly sensitive to that experience. But music cannot go very far back in time and explore creatively a distant past: its instruments and materials are not as permanent as a written page. Music is vulnerable. We can read, translate, and discuss Homer in depth, but we can only theorize or barely imagine how Greek music was, because we have never heard it.

In the Middle Ages, profane melodies were often transcribed for liturgical purposes; transcription in music played also a substantial, mnemonic role. Countless folk melodies made their way across Europe, transforming themselves and turning up in the most unlikely places. From the thirteenth century on, an increasingly codified musical notation—which is itself a form of transcription—had profoundly influenced the spread of music, both publicly and privately, and favored a growing exchange of musical ideas from country to country. During the fifteenth and sixteenth centuries instrumental music rapidly acquired its own status as a transcription of vocal music, becoming an extension of it. The practice of transcribing parts from a vocal polyphony for a solo instrument (the lute, for example) was fundamental in the process of giving birth to accompanied melody.

"This *Ritornello* was played by two ordinary violins," Monteverdi writes in the score of his *Orfeo*, documenting the first performance but also suggesting, with that past tense, that on another occasion different instruments might well have been used. Until Beethoven, any acknowledged musical form was a quotation and a commentary, hence a form of transcription. A gigue was a legitimate inhabitant of a suite; the vast range of transcriptions and transformations through which the formal dance model (the gigue) together with its occasional container (the suite) underwent, from the sixteenth century to Schoenberg, is very significant. This is to say that musical transcription, seen from a historical perspective, implies not only interpretation but also evolutionary and transformational processes. The practice, the possibilities, and the needs of transcription were an organic part of musical invention and also a natural step in the professional development of a musician.

Copying, the simplest form of transcription, was an important learning experience: the very young Mozart would copy whatever Leopold suggested, and later in his life, he transcribed Handel's *Messiah* and Bach's fugues. It seems that Schubert copied Beethoven's Second Symphony, and Beethoven copied a few of Mozart's string quartets, parts of *Don Giovanni, The Magic Flute,* and the *Requiem,* and transcribed for himself a vocal fugue from the *Messiah.* Brahms copied Schubert's lieder. Copying, like transcription, implies some sort of identification with the copied or transcribed text, and also an act of generosity. Walter Benjamin said that there is "a kind of saintly vocation in the sheer act of copying" and that "the power of a text is different when it is read from when it is copied out. . . . Copying is to *be* the text being copied." I think that the act of copying by Schubert, Beethoven, Brahms, and many others can be seen as inhabited by the same emotions.

During the Baroque period, when musical roles and hierarchies were part of a rather stable and unifying conceptual framework, vocal technique began to assimilate the modes and manners of instrumental music. The relative homogeneity of the techniques and their highly codified notation made it possible to transfer music from one set of instruments to another. Over the centuries, the progressive diffusion of printed musical scores, and of transcriptions, generated countless mysteries that would have taxed even Sherlock Holmes. A notorious example is J. S. Bach's exceedingly well-known Toccata and Fugue in D minor for organ. Its authenticity has been questioned by recent scholarship (an original solo violin piece later transcribed for the organ, neither by Bach, is one of the hypotheses suggested), raising a whole range of stylistic and notational issues that reveal the complexity of the Baroque practice of copying and transcription. Bach was constantly transcribing himself as well as Vivaldi, Pergolesi, and other contemporaries. Bach's Chaconne from the Partita in D Major for solo violin was transcribed dozens of times in the nineteenth century—for small and large orchestras, for piano, for guitar, and so on. Schumann added a piano accompaniment to it, and Brahms turned it into a left-hand piano study.

As in music, in all languages there are translations that are copies, translations that are "faithful portraits," and paraphrases that are a travesty of the original. There are translations which germanize the French original, or americanize the Italian, and vice versa. But this is a small price to pay for the privilege of having Goethe on French bookshelves, Shakespeare in Italy, or Proust in America. Then there are literary works which are virtual translations from the outset, because they are impregnated with the stylistic, conceptual, and rhetorical peculiarities of other languages, traditions, or translations. This is particularly true of children's literature and of the more stereotyped forms of nineteenth-century opera librettos.

But there are also literary works which resist translation; they may only be interpreted, paraphrased, described, or commented upon. These include Mallarmé's *Le Livre* and Joyce's *Finnegans Wake*. Any attempt at translating these would be distinctly difficult, if not impossible or pointless. The reasons for this impossibility have something in common with music. In *Finnegans Wake* the symbolism, the syntax, phonetics, iconic imagery, and gestural content create a series of semantic short circuits, a polyphony of associations that leave no leeway whatsoever for alternative expressions or enunciations. Moreover, Joyce develops and exhibits a language that seems to want to assimilate the molecules of all languages. In this complex and lush landscape, the old Saussurian signifier and signified tend to be one and the same. The same thing often happens in the music of the twentieth century—aware as it is of its past history, yet eager to detach itself from it—where a transcription would become an improper and even destructive act. To translate Joyce's *Finnegans Wake*, Mallarmé's *Le Livre*, or the poetry of e. e. cummings would be like transcribing Debussy's *Jeux*, Bartók's *Music for Strings, Percussion, and Celesta*, Boulez's *Marteau sans Maître*, Carter's Double Concerto, Stockhausen's *Gruppen*, or most of my own works. It would be like carrying out a completely arbitrary operation on works whose meaning lies, among other things, in the interaction of their acoustic components, in their musical characterization and functions, in their specific sound relationships, and in the "thematization" of those relationships.

Transcription was—and still is, at times—an instrument of popularization. In the early nineteenth century music was made known principally through four-hands piano transcriptions, a decidedly less passive but also less accurate equivalent of today's CDs and radio broadcasts. Adaptations and transcriptions were part of the currency—sometimes a counterfeit part—in the big business of Italian melodrama. Franz Liszt's piano transcriptions and paraphrases, addressed to a cosmopolitan socialite public, contributed immensely to the evolution of piano technique and greatly furthered musical exchange, even though they have little bearing on the stature of Liszt as a composer.

Transcription has often been used, at least partially, to comment upon and to assimilate elements from past and foreign experiences. This is why it is so difficult, sometimes, to assign precise borders to the vast territories of transcription. The embittered, jostling expressive "objects" that populate Mahler's world and, from a very different perspective, the direct references to real-life sounds in the visionary musical documentaries of Charles Ives are significant examples of commentary and assimilation as an indirect form of transcription.

Then there is Schoenberg who, to our great relief, transcribed for orchestra his *Theme and Variations,* op. 43 (originally for wind instruments). He also transcribed—though in a problematic way—Brahms, Bach, Handel, and Mahler. With Webern, on the other hand, transcription became a form of analysis—as is the case with his version of Bach's six-part Ricercare from the *Musical Offering* and the impressive "Brahmsian" transcription for piano quintet of Schoenberg's Chamber Symphony, op. 9. This is a case where transcription becomes a transparent act of love and learning.

As for Ravel, his transcriptions, where the piano is transcended into the orchestra, are all very well known. Stravinsky's transcriptions covered a very wide and complex territory. Think of the different versions of *Les Noces,* and think of *Agon,* which is a kind of synthetic transcription (almost a parody) of a large segment of music history. The young Stockhausen showed his musical coming-of-age by transcribing his *Kontra-punkte* from a huge, uncontrolled orchestra to ten solo instruments. With Mauricio Kagel transcription becomes parody, commentary upon everything he encounters. Boulez's transcriptions and re-transcriptions of his own works (such as *Notations* for orchestra, where he uncovers, transcribes, and amplifies several short piano pieces written forty-five years earlier) are an important aspect of his creative process and of his proliferating vision.

I too have transcribed a great deal. Except when there are specific practical or personal reasons, my transcriptions are invariably prompted by analytical considerations. I have always thought that the best possible commentary on a symphony is another symphony, and I reckon that the third part of my *Sinfonia* is the best and deepest analysis that I could have hoped to make of the Scherzo from Mahler's Second Symphony. The same is true of my *Rendering* for orchestra, which is my own act of love for Schubert and for his sketches for his last unfinished symphony in D major (D936A), which occupied him during the final weeks of his life. With my transcription for orchestra of Mahler's youthful *Lieder,* for instance, I wanted to bring to light the undercurrents of the original piano part: Wagner, Brahms, the adult Mahler, and the modes of orchestration that came after him.

But let's step outside the catalogue of more or less explicit forms of transcription. Let's consider, for instance, a *concertante* situation, in which a soloist coexists with his own image reflected and transcribed into an orchestra which may become a sort of distorting and amplifying mirror of it (this interaction can undergo interesting developments also with computer-assisted technologies). We can imagine *concertante* forms bringing to the surface, transcribing, and amplifying functions which are hidden and embedded in a pre-existing and self-sufficient instrumental solo. It is as if one were dealing with a natural, pre-existing structure, and sought to extract inherent forms and hidden patterns. This attitude has nothing in common with Schoenberg's curious procedure of writing a rather indifferent piano part to his *Fantasia,* op. 47, after having written out the violin part in full; but it does, ideally, with the work of Paul Klee and his creative interaction with nature, a work that constantly comments on the roots of its own becoming.

The series of my *Chemins* for soloist and orchestra (or instrumental group) elaborate on previous, independent solo pieces such as some of my *Sequenze*. These *Chemins* do not offer a transcription of a solo part composed at an earlier date—which does not in fact undergo any modification whatsoever—but rather an exposition and an amplification of what is implicit, hidden, so to speak, in that solo part. In the case of *Chemins I,* based on *Sequenza II* for harp, there is a very differentiated repartee between the soloist and the added instrumental forces (an orchestra and two more harps), and between the multiple perspectives of listening imposed by these new forces on the original solo *Sequenza.* The linear development in the orchestra and the triangular interaction of the three harps keep the natural amplification transparent even in moments of extreme density. This process of amplification involves different and simultaneous layers of articulation and different modes of performance, all engaged in the same sequential, harmonic journey from sound to noise. The harp in fact is often transformed into a noise generator: it does not evoke the pretty delicacies of the French school but, maybe, the noises of an unlikely forest. Nevertheless, the orchestra and the two harps reply to the soloist, often echoing it in a cause-and-effect kind of relation.

The situation is reversed in *Chemins III* (on *Chemins II*), for

viola, a group of ten instruments, and orchestra. Here everything coexists; there is no dialogue, no cause-and-effect relation,
but duplication and simultaneous reinforcement. The solo part
(Sequenza VI) mirrors itself, rather faithfully, in the different
instrumental layers. There are varying degrees of fusion among
the different instrumental forces, based on harmonic characters
and speed of articulation. There is an interaction between periodic and discontinuous, almost random, patterns that will ori-
ent our perception of the phasing and dephasing of the various
frequency bands. At the same time, the instrumental group and
the orchestra are amplifying a global aspect of this work which
moves, in a rather discontinuous way, from noise to sound.
The sequence of works—*Sequenza VI* for viola, *Chemins II* for
ten instruments, and *Chemins III*—are in search of a melody,
going through different subtractive steps. When the melody is
finally about to take shape, the work ends. Naturally.

Chemins IV for oboe and eleven strings, based on my *Sequenza VII* for oboe, develops a still different form of interaction and transcription. A single, isolated note of the oboe is
repeated, always in the same register, through an almost regu-
lar sequence of accents and silences. The same note is developed in the instrumental group, undergoing a constant variation of timbre and dynamics for the entire duration of the

composition. Always present and always different, that note acts as a generalized tonic or like the vanishing point in a landscape. It enables us to perceive and compare the smallest oscillations of color, intensity, and intonation. At times our vanishing point is lost in a cumulative process; or it is no longer heard as such because it is absorbed, like an overtone, as a structural part of a harmonic process. The ever-present pitch at times is forgotten and at other times is recognized and remembered. The articulations of the soloist are alternatively extended, prepared, or unexpectedly foreshadowed by the instrumental group, creating a dialogue of "mobilities" and "immobilities," of "befores" and "afters," of "memories" and "forgetfulness." They look ahead, they look behind, and naturally they always look at each other. The dialogue stops once this process has proliferated so far that the instrumental group now functions as an echo-chamber, filled with fragments deduced from everything that we have heard so far, while the soloist's original physiognomy is completely transformed.

A dialogue between a pre-existing musical text and the otherness of an added text can therefore be developed through multiple forms of interaction, from the most unanimous to the most conflictual and estranged. But it is exactly through these moments of estrangement that a deep connection with the initial data, with the given material of the solo instrument, will be both challenged and justified. By "initial data" I don't necessarily mean something that comes earlier in time. It is possible to develop *concertante* situations in which the solo instrument becomes a generator of functions that are entrusted to the instrumental group, which in turn generates the solo part; thus the group generates something that already existed, in such a way that the solo is no longer a generator but a result.

This implies the possibility of transforming and even abusing the text's integrity so as to perform an act of constructive demolition on it. Transcription seems to get drawn into the very core of the formative process, taking joint and full responsibility for the structural definition of the work. It is not the sound that is being transcribed, therefore, but the idea.

I feel that the implications of this proceeding, although quickly described, can be quite far-reaching. This is a position that we can also adopt with regard to history, not just musical history; in this perspective we are invited to renew our perception of history, maybe to re-invent it so that, fully responsible, we can accept the idea of a history that is exploring us and we can give ourselves, again and again, the possibility of remembering the future.

The history of vocal music is also the history of translation of a text into music. Think of the text of the Mass, which has been sung in different ways, with different music, who knows how many times. Not only the Eucharist but also a poem by Heine, Goethe, or Mallarmé is structurally and semantically modified and renewed, at least in part, when it is explored and absorbed into music by Schubert, Schumann, Debussy, Ravel, Boulez, or others. If a musical thought is to manifest itself in full in relation to a text, it must be able to modify that text, to carry out an analytical transformation of it, while of course remaining conditioned by it. This will at least prevent the well-known and passive situation, so common in today's commercially oriented music, of a text that becomes a pretext in a stereotyped musical context.

Vocal technique plays a concrete but somehow ambiguous part in the transformation of a text into music. Even the epoch-making Sprechstimme, conceived by Schoenberg for *Pierrot Lunaire,* is a meaningful and unique case of vocal ambiguity. In the vocal part we hear the gestures of Berlin cabaret (maybe), as well as the mannerism of Franco-German melodrama (certainly) and the Liederkreis tradition. We can listen to it also as an exalted recitation or as a pauperized song—or both.

Even in the vocal music of the highest and most subtle conformity of music and poetry (I am thinking of the German lied), when we seem to experience the miracle of a quasi-spontaneous formal and expressive agreement between musical and poetic structure, we are aware of diverging relations, of expressive disagreements, between musical and poetic design, between musical and poetic strophes, meter and rhyme, between modes and moods. For instance, the journey toward madness and oblivion in Schubert's *Winterreise* is also a journey toward an increasing presence of translucent major keys.

To look for specific and obstinate confirmations of common intents between music and poetry in the romantic lied can become a futile operation, since the cultural criteria involved in themselves guarantee a relative code of reciprocity between text and music. Codes, methods, and theories are everywhere, in a given cultural frame. They are obviously very present and active in vocal music, where a composer interfaces two dimensions that imply, in any case, possibilities of logical inferences and a substantial degree of probabilities in relation to the premises. I think that even in the highest moments of the German lied experience (*Dichterliebe* by Schumann, for instance), it can be more rewarding to unglue the music from the text rather than relying on obvious or specious observations that end up transforming a lied into a Rorschach inkblot.

Henri Pousseur has achieved a deep structural study of the complex spiral of harmonic and key relations in *Dichterliebe,* bringing to light, as he says, "a global structure of remarkable coherence and complexity. Behind a varied texture there is a unified material that traverses the sixteen pieces in a way that never happened before in any form of vocal music made of diversified, collected moments." But, let me add, there are also moments of significant divarication between the music and the poem. The musical episodes and the narrative itinerary of Schumann's selection of Heine's poems seem, at the end of the cycle, to close up and sink together, holding themselves tight, with ironic dignity, in the waters of a romantic renunciation. Nevertheless, in the last song there is something that stays afloat: it is the closing comment of the piano where, evoking and developing the last measures of two previous songs, the musician talks directly to the poet, inviting him, with benevolent, friendly, and moving expression, not to take himself too seriously. This way of "stepping out" of the poet's coffin, this brief and musically self-sufficient meditation, seems to imply a step toward transcendence of emotions.

In 1965, right here in Cambridge, I had my first encounter with Roman Jakobson at Harvard's Faculty Club. He came toward me with those bushy, glinting eyes of his and asked me point-blank: "So, Berio, what is music?" After a moment of baffled silence, I replied that music is everything we listen to with the intention of listening to music, and that anything can *become* music.

I've always been faithful to this spur-of-the-moment reply—if not in practice, at least as an ideal. I can now qualify it by adding that anything can become music as long as it can be musically conceptualized, as long as it can be translated into different dimensions. Such conception, such translation is possible only within the notion of music as Text, a multi-dimensional Text that is in continuous evolution.

Jakobson in fact had already stated something of the kind when he wrote that the entire apparatus of language—with its linguistic, phonetic, phonological, rhetorical, and syntactical dimensions—contributes to the poetic process, not just verse, meter, rhyme, symmetry, and so on. By this he implied that the priorities of poetic and, in our case, musical functions have to be selected and recombined each time around. He gave the well-known example of a missionary in Africa trying to convince members of a local community not to go around naked. "But you're naked, too," replied a tribesman, pointing at the missionary's face. "But only my face is naked," said the missionary, to which the candid reply was: "Well, for us the face is all over!"

The most significant vocal music of the last few decades has been investigating exactly that: the possibility of exploring and absorbing musically the full face of language. Stepping out of the purely syllabic articulation of a text, vocal music can deal with the totality of its configurations, including the phonetic one and including the ever-present vocal gestures. It can be useful for a composer to remember that the sound of a voice is always a quotation, always a gesture. The voice, whatever it does, even the simplest noise, is inescapably meaningful: it always triggers associations and it always carries within itself a model, whether natural or cultural.

Music, I suppose, will never retreat from words, and neither will words retreat from music. Words on music can themselves become a sort of transcription of musical thinking. However, at times music seems to be surrounded by a Muzak of verbalism. Beautiful and ugly, music and non-music, tonal and atonal, closed and open, formal and informal, spoken and sung, traditional and modern, free and strict are certainly all legitimate and conventional terms. But musical experience seems always ready to contradict what is said about it, particularly when this is expressed in peremptory terms, with the rather moralistic slant of binary conflicts. The dilemmas provoked by binary oppositions can lead us to ask ourselves if musical experience is more significant than the argument it prompts. Or whether the dimension of concrete experience and the dimension of the discourse which translates the experience into words are perhaps interchangeable. But we are also led to think that a conflict or contradiction has no point because music cannot be true or untrue the way a discourse can. It cannot, as a behavior, be either good or bad. Nor can it be reduced to a "thing," or to a procedure that is open to manipulation by a discourse. It is a vicious circle. Discourses on music do not perturb us—or we wouldn't be here now—but we know that music can occasionally perturb us when, loaded with meanings, it begs to be spoken about, questioned, and related to an elusive *elsewhere*. Formerly, this contradictory *elsewhere* could be identified with a universal concept of art which also accommodated music, though like an unwanted and defaulting tenant. But the notion of art tends to transform itself into the *artistic:* it tends to recognize itself more in a diffuse cloud of feelings than in a specific work. We find art everywhere and nowhere—perhaps because it has lost one of its most powerful propellants: that of turning against itself.

The musical work seems to need the constant reassurance of a verbal discourse that would act as a mediator between its outer form and its essence. This is even more true when the direct experience of a musical work is not easily connected with that familiar and conciliatory notion of art, or with the common belief that the music we listen to has something to do with what we feel and therefore could say about it. There are times when the translation of music into words seems to substitute for direct experience. But since music's more salient and enduring contents are above all conceptual, this substitution is meaningful only if the words actually contribute to outlining the process of thought that underlies an experience that tends to be free of verbal associations.

A discourse on music can become a substitute for musical creativity when it strays into areas which music itself cannot knowingly enter. In this way a new poetics of musical hermeneutics and aesthetics takes shape, something which Adorno took to extreme heights. Adorno's complex, polyphonic, and polysemic discourse on music—with his characteristic thought cells that multiply into lofty thought systems—left a significant legacy of ideas and questions for two generations of musicians. Adorno taught us how to analyze practical experience dialectically but at the same time to keep our distance from it. It is a bit like being tied, with ears wide open, to the mast of an extremely provocative intellectual ship, without being lured onto the rocks by the Sirens.

It is the *elsewhere* of musical discourse, rather than practical experience, which has taught us that something "ugly" can be more dignified and useful than something "beautiful" or "aesthetically correct." It has taught us that every creative act involves reflection, and that it is necessary to distinguish between "implicit" theory, which includes composition as a form of thought "in" music, and "explicit" theory, which is a reflection "on" music, and helps us to understand (I am quoting Carl Dahlhaus) "to what extent a thought—that is, a discourse—'on' music is useful and indispensable to the thought 'in' music inherent to every composition, or, on the contrary, to what extent it is a superfluous addition to an autonomous practice of composing which is alone in its decisions."

With this I have attempted to describe certain twists and turns of a labyrinth which, in my view, offers only one way out: comprehension implies translation. We could fill pages and pages with descriptions of behavior and conceptual paradigms which, combined with a detailed analysis of concrete experience (exactly what type of analysis is always an open question), could perhaps contribute to a coherently ramified vision of the translation of music into words. But I am not too convinced that this operation could produce satisfactory results, given the constant evolution of the phenomena in question. Given, on the other hand, the impoverishing tendencies in the musical scene today, it is difficult to decide what kind of satisfaction we could hope to gain by it. Maybe we have to make do with knowing that there are structures of thought "on" music that interact with each other (such as those of Adorno and Dahlhaus): veritable para-musical constructions, which have influenced thought "in" music no less than the music composed over the same period did. These complex forms of translation of musical experience have their own value and import, as poetics that create a sort of music of meanings. In this respect, Adorno's "The Essay as Form" and his studies on Schubert and Mahler are superior examples. Without overlooking the specific musical details, and while evaluating them technically in a very penetrating way, Adorno constructs an edifice of thought that reflects our (essentially spiritual) desire to go musically to and fro across those wide spaces between social process and individual progress, and between the (often seductive) outward form of that gap and its (always enigmatic) essence.

When we are dealing with a set of culturally homogeneous interests that are familiar to us, we tend to identify ourselves with the objects of our interest. Transcribing or analyzing the work of others, in Europe or America, is always a bit like talking about ourselves. But now and then we want to venture into distant cultural territories and explore different cultural identities. When this world of ours, with its need for appropriating everything around it, comes into contact with music and musical rituals that are fixed in time (fixed like the social structures that produced them), then the chances of our being able to truly identify with them are drastically reduced. This foray into musical domains that are heavily determined by performance techniques, harmonies, melodies, heterophonies, and rhythms can trigger an illusory sense of identification.

The pretense of total identification is, to my mind, one of the most sterile forms of contact with another culture. Total identification implies some kind of spontaneity that, in this case, would only be superficially emotive because it would be deprived of any profound form of cultural rigor. Frankly, I would find it hard to identify with the behavior of a Tibetan monk, and none of you, I suppose, could quite put yourselves into the shoes of a Sicilian fisherman. But there are rare and precious cases in which identification and detachment coexist creatively hand-in-hand. Béla Bartók is one of the most significant and complex examples of musical bilingualism. Between the world of melodies, rhythms, metrics, and folk harmonies that Bartók was exploring and the world of "cultivated" music in which he developed, there is an indissoluble and profound relationship that is an integral part of Bartók's creativity. In the development of large forms, Bartók, rather than transcribing folk melodies, transcribes their inherent, implicit meaning. Therefore, in most cases he invents them. Furthermore, Bartók develops a dialogue between the original peasant musical materials and a formal construction (whether an "arched" one based on "golden section" proportions, or one based on "axial" harmonic procedures) that keeps them organically and morphologically distinct, yet structurally inseparable—a true fusion, an amalgam of seemingly disparate structuring elements, and not merely an emulsion ready for all uses.

Bartók certainly doesn't serve up some musical sightseeing tour of Transylvania or a postcard of the Romanian countryside. In many cases the source material already offers a rich and fecund seedbed of ambiguity. For example, the first five notes of *Music for Strings, Percussion, and Celesta* crop up, by mere coincidence, in Webern's *Variations,* op. 30; four of these same notes make up the famous melodic cell on the name B-A-C-H; and the first three are the *incipit* of a Hungarian folksong. So we have four cultural seeds, so to speak, all contained in the same five notes, seeds which germinate and multiply in the four sections of Bartók's remarkable work, in which latent and manifest meaning, the parts and the whole, all interact in a wholly novel and transparent way. It may be that Bartók's explicit nature, his apparent innocence and his complex relationship with history and with the cultural realities around him, prevented Adorno and Dahlhaus from accepting him into their solemn intellectual architectures. Adorno's silence on Bartók is significant; it reveals the dogmatic side of his fundamental Theory of Aesthetics and his difficulty in dealing with diversities.

If we step outside our cultural sphere and go to Africa, say, the scene changes considerably. We come across music that cannot be listened to with the ears of someone who wants at all cost to write it out on the staff. It is essential that Western musicians approach these musical behaviors with intelligent and sensitive ears, in order to grasp the sophisticated processes behind what may seem to be merely blowing pipes and hitting stones and drums. In this way we can discover some remarkable new things that come from far outside our own sphere, but can nevertheless touch us deeply. Appropriating them with the intellectual tools of our music no longer needs to be a matter of cultural colonialism but can be an act of awareness and respect, of love, for cultural identities which can also tell us something about ourselves.

In central Africa there is a small, pacific community which we would define as "highly musical," if the members of the community had our notion of music. The tribe, known as the Banda Linda, was studied by the ethnomusicologist Simha Arom. In groups of about forty, the members of the tribe play long wooden pipes, each of which produces a single note. Each note is repeated on a single rhythmic module, with occasional slight variations that do not affect the "block" character of the whole. When all the players blow into their instruments, they produce an altogether new sound—new to western ears. It is both complex and coordinated, something between a cathedral of sound and an implacable musical machine. The playing of the Banda Linda wooden horns is governed by an infrangible principle. There is a pentatonic melody which is not actually played by any one person: its notes are distributed among the players through a register of approximately two octaves. As if by some tacit social agreement, nobody plays the melody as such, yet its nature and its spirit are ever-present at any point in this fabulous sound "installation."

It goes without saying that I studied and adapted the procedure involved not because I wanted to transcribe the Banda

Linda's heterophonies for a symphony orchestra or for the piano, but because I wanted to transfer the principle, the idea, into other dimensions of music, and also to extend the same principle to other cultures (Sicily, Slovenia, Scotland, and so forth). In *Coro* (the work which I derived from that complex experience) I had the Banda Linda idiom come a very long way, interacting with the musical procedures and techniques of other cultures, adapting and transforming the original musical functions of their "sound machine."

But, without knowing it, the Banda Linda themselves had already traveled a long way. That process of segmentation, subdivision, and rhythmic distribution of the melody had already been tried out in Europe in the thirteenth and fourteenth centuries with the *hoquetus* (hocket), which involved the jerky rhythmic fragmentation of a given melody among two or three voices—a well-known pre-polyphonic technique of composition which also tended to give the melody a further form of temporal organization. It is very interesting indeed to find that the ancient, unchanging African heterophonies that belong to an oral tradition can be correlated through an analogous principle of performance with an important stepping-stone in the continuously evolving written tradition of European music.

I do not believe that Adam, in that famous garden, ever received the divine gift of a universal musical grammar, eventually doomed to destruction in the Tower of Babel. However that may be, in closing this second lecture I would like to say that these remarks have been like putting a message in a bottle and casting it out to sea—a cautious, circumspect message. Now and then music sends out hesitant cues as to the existence of innate organisms which, if fittingly translated and interpreted, may help us pinpoint the embryos of a universal musical grammar. I do not think that such a discovery can be useful to musical creativity, nor to the utopian prospect of a perfect, common musical language that will enable musicians to speak and be unanimously spoken. But I do think that it could contribute to exploring musical experience as a "language of languages," establishing a constructive interchange between diverse cultures and a peaceful defense of those diversities. I hope so. In the meantime, we'll keep translating.

3

FORGETTING MUSIC

There are a thousand ways of forgetting music, and I am mostly interested in the active ways of forgetting rather than the passive and unconscious ways. In other words, I am interested in voluntary amnesias, although the desire to possess and remember the history of all times and all places is an integral part of modern thought, and the practical means of satisfying this desire are certainly available in our day and age.

Today, the listener has a tendency to make use of the whole of past music as if it were a consumer commodity. This makes sense because for the listener the past is the most available resource of musical knowledge, although this tendency often carries the signs of an unconscious ideological frustration, since it is rooted not in a plausible code of musical values but in the way we are conditioned by the market.

A sociology of conservation, of hoarding, of musical avarice and fetishism has already been written by Adorno, in a different time, when it was the right thing to do, when an analysis of the listener and of listening implied a moral, if not a political, judgment.

The conservation of the past makes sense because even the most unprepared listener is aware that music cannot be hung on the wall. Music is performed, is constantly in motion, forever "in progress," especially since there is nothing really permanent to guarantee continuity between the mind of a composer and the hands of a performer, between the musical structure and the levels of articulation, as they are heard.

But conservation of the past also makes sense in a negative way, becoming a way of forgetting music. It provides listeners with an illusion of continuity; it gives them the illusion of being free to select what appears to confirm that continuity, as well as the illusion of being free to censure everything that appears to upset it. This is why musical performance often seems to have autonomous life: it becomes a sort of merchandise, indifferent to the music it is supposed to be serving. However diversified these kinds of performing life appear to be, they are all deeply rooted, I insist, in a conditioning consumer society rather than in the world of ideas.

Performance techniques, musical instruments, and performing spaces are also shrines to memory, as much and often more so than musical works in themselves. The modes and places of performance have evolutionary timings that are different and frequently independent of those of the musical text. The performers of the seventeenth, eighteenth, and part of the nineteenth centuries lived in the present. They had no cumbersome philological ambitions, nor were they concerned, as a rule, with an accumulated legacy of technique, instruments, and places of performance.

The first public concert halls, built in Europe and England in the late eighteenth and early nineteenth century, served as a confirmation of the astonishing fact that music was democratically available to everybody, but also that it had become a consumer good, available to anyone who could afford its price. The concert hall was already a museum: it allowed the accumulation of musical properties and catered to the desire for memory and immortality. Bach wrote, so to speak, "disposable" cantatas, whereas the musical works of the Romantics were fighting the passing time, expecting a guarantee of eternity. Maybe the need to remember and possess history is also the expression of an obscure cultural—perhaps we might call it a religious—conflict: between music as an expression of an immortal world inhabited by mortal individuals, and music in a society of immortal souls dwelling in a mortal world.

Today we live with calendars at hand but, at the same time, we live with the feeling that everything in history occurs without particular regard for its chronology, and that even music is a sort of warehouse of samples, whose shelf life—whose relative permanence or oblivion, whose chronological placement—is ultimately irrelevant because, when we get down to it, it can be pushed around according to our inner needs and desires as listeners, performers, and composers. When this happens, we realize that the shelves of our musical space imply that the past and future, the "before" and "after," are relative and even interchangeable entities. The analogy may be risky, but I still remember my surprise—a long time ago, when I was still in high school—on reading Plutarch's *Parallel Lives,* to see the author narrate the birth, life, thought, and death of an important figure from Greek history and compare it, side by side, with one from Roman history. There is no reference to dates. The figures may have lived five hundred years apart (like Aristides and Caesar), yet there is no reference to the calendar.

My point is not to celebrate the relevance of Plutarch's values to the musical scene of our time, but to stress the fact that in order to get a true sense of musical evolution, we must detach ourselves from a linear and irreversible view of historical time. It is precisely this detachment that allows us, on occasion, to forget or to attribute different and even conflicting values to musical works that detach themselves from the passing time. The history of vocal music and music-theater of the eighteenth and nineteenth centuries, after all, can be written without taking account of Monteverdi, but that of the twentieth century cannot. The history of late eighteenth-century music can be written without mentioning Bach, but that of the past two centuries cannot. The deep meaning of Mahler's music became evident only fifty years after his death.

We are experiencing a twilight of the distinction between long-term and short-term memory, between before and after. Everything, in that fading light, appears to become useful and intrinsically complementary. In the light of that dusk, the most radically different options coexist: Mendelssohn "discovers" Bach; music philology is born; history becomes a science, while composers and listeners alike begin to elaborate a selective memory that isolates single works from the circumstances of their origins.

However, it is also in that light that the virtuoso performer becomes more aware of the past as something to be exploited, and becomes more forgetful of the fact that the only form of virtuosity worthy of the name is virtuosity of intelligence, capable of penetrating and rendering different musical worlds. We all know by now that a pianist who claims to be a "specialist" in the Classical or Romantic repertory, and who is playing Beethoven or Chopin without having had the need of experiencing the music of the twentieth century, is just as shallow as a pianist who claims to be a "specialist" in contemporary music but whose hands and mind have never been traversed, on a profound level, by Beethoven or Chopin.

The increasing diversity of the forms of musical consumption, the evolution of techniques and audiences, and the consequent instability of possible points of reference are the product, to a certain extent, of the available means of recording, reproducing, and conserving music. Such is the quantity of noise—actual and virtual—around us, that it cannot be made the object of a methodological analysis. It is not so much a musical phenomenon as a phenomenon of acoustic amnesia that has nothing to do with any musically valuable territory we are interested in exploring. If Walter Benjamin were still among us, he would have nothing to worry about, he could set his mind at rest: the same means that contribute to the reproducibility of the work, and hence to the crisis of its authority, its authenticity, its "aura," may perhaps be the very means that contribute in the future to a different definition of its authority, its authenticity, its "aura."

Through new technologies, one can enter new acoustic and musical dimensions. Already in the 1950s Karlheinz Stockhausen, with *Zeitmasse, Gruppen, Kontakte,* and the related theoretical apparatus (*wie die Zeit vergeht,* "how time passes"), was looking for an extreme, and often paradoxical, conceptual homogeneity among qualitative and quantitative sound dimensions, among time proportions, frequency, and timbre, among micro- and macrophenomena and forms, in the attempt to reach a quasi-natural, quasi-divine, total fusion of all possible qualitative and quantitative parameters. We know, however, that in nature every morphogenesis has a molecular basis, while in music—vocal and instrumental—the integration of large- and small-scale phenomena is never innocent because the phenomena have no absolute values. Through the new computer-assisted technologies the composer deals with, so to speak, "molecular," digitized sound dimensions where everything can be formed and transformed, where anything can become anything else. However, this fascinating field of possibilities is also very risky, when the computer loses contact with the specificity of the musical matter.

We can refuse history, but we cannot forget about it, even with the new technologies, when we deal with sound "molecules," even when we digitally design new sounds or when we synthesize or hybridize familiar sounds that do not carry with them traces of musical usage. Music can explore, meaningfully, new and uncharted territories when it acts like a movie camera—focusing, analyzing the sound subject—and when the composer, like a movie director, decides the angles, the speed, the close-ups, the zooms, the blow-ups, the editing, and the silences. And this can be done without a computer, especially when the sound subject is the human voice, which, by its very nature, is overloaded with traces of musical and non-musical experiences and lived-in associations.

In the previous lecture I suggested, quoting Roman Jakobson, that the musical potential of the voice is everywhere, in all of its articulatory features, in all of its gestures. Musically, a voice is not only a noble instrument; it is also the sum of all its aspects and behaviors, from the most respectable to the most trivial, and the most estranged from music. In coughing, for instance, there is no trace of music, but nevertheless I believe that we can endow daily vocal behaviors with musical sense, just as everyday motions of the body can be developed choreographically.

Let us imagine a sequence—a loop—of continuously changing basic vocal gestures (laughter, sobbing, crying, coughing, and so forth)—vocal stereotypes that are not normally associated with musical experiences. They can be made to interact by the use of combinatorial criteria involving gestures and techniques, as well as positioning of vocal resonance, speed and nature of the articulations, and so forth. A woman laughing, for example, can have something in common with the performance of a coloratura soprano. The vocal events on this loop have different degrees of association, and laughter, for instance, can become the main generating factor in a discontinuous vocal landscape which, however, still lacks the most challenging and intense gesture: words. Therefore, let us also imagine an elementary text composed of short modular sentences, of recurring interchangeable flashes of meaning, evocative of a potential narrative that unfolds with various degrees of discontinuity. The text loop and the loop of vocal gestures have different lengths, and turn like two circles of different diameters which revolve at different speeds and never meet twice at the same point. This is what happens in my *Sequenza III* for solo voice.

To control and convey musical coherence to such a vast set of vocal behaviors, it is necessary to apply to the text combinatorial criteria that are analogous to those applied to the vocal gestures: it is necessary to break up the text, to demolish it (at least apparently), to scatter the fragments on different levels so that they can be reassembled and recomposed in a musical, rather than a discursive or narrative, perspective. Thus segmented, broken up, and permutated, the text will never be perceived in its entirety. The vocal gesture, which can capture attention as a coded and iconic form of communication, loaded with associations, is contradicted by the relative indifference of the text and by its contiguity with other equally indifferent gestures. The text is in turn "disturbed" by gestures and by a mode of delivery that can only simulate an interpretation of the text in a sort of conflictual relationship. This multiple and somehow alienated relationship between text and vocal gesture (which continually destroy and reconstruct each other), and the interpreter's desperate attempt to tackle the intrusive and unarrestable vocal kaleidoscope of associations, can confer a tragicomic slant on the performance, as if it were at the same time the parody and the translation of something elusive, something absent.

In *Sequenza III* there are certain curious absences. The work has no memory of vocal music; it lacks linguistic autonomy because there is no possibility of linear comprehension of the text. It lacks a specifically musical autonomy because the meaning of the event lies in the everyday vocal gestures; consequently, it lacks a reference to the complex history of reciprocal formalizations which, in the history of our vocal music, marks the relationship between text and music. These absences, I feel, are an invitation to listen afresh, and to witness that miraculous spectacle of sound becoming sense—perhaps a sense that we have not encountered before: an invitation to follow the transition from unrelated vocal sounds and gestures to a meaningful state of urgency. Something meaningless doesn't make any sense, but something that doesn't make any sense can be meaningful; without this basic awareness, there would be little point in developing, extracting, and inventing musical experiences from the total face (to use Jakobson's image) of a vocal sound body.

A musical work is never alone—it always has a big family to cope with, and it must be capable of living many lives; it can be left to its own past, and it must be capable of living in the present in a variety of ways, at times forgetful of its origins. In the light of these and other conditions, the history of western music appears only occasionally to pay attention to its chronological sequence. Indifferent to the fires in its libraries, it seems, at times, to invent its own calendars, so that the distinction between the often vague directions of historical becoming and the constellation of works shaping our aesthetic experience is a metaphysical dichotomy detached from reality. It is this detachment that allows us to perform a salutary manipulation of our memory, without having to pay duty at the roadblocks, along the imaginary borderline separating the past from the present. If we accept the terms of this separation, we might as well place our trust in the voice of ordinary common sense and, without having to drag Plutarch into it, recall what historians have told us over and over again: that failure to understand the present has its roots in ignorance of the past, and that it is useless to struggle to understand the past without an adequate knowledge of the present.

The whole of musical experience, even in its most concrete forms, is permeated with this elementary paradigm. I often find myself in the position of trying, reluctantly, to counteract a dialectical mode of thought which implies a binary and moralistic division of musical experience. I say "reluctantly" because it was this school of thought (I'm talking once more about Adorno) that provided us with the most far-reaching and penetrating conceptual instruments that musical culture has had at its disposal in the twentieth century—but at the same time the most dogmatic.

I don't think any experience in music has been the object of so many passionate ideological attacks as Stravinsky's neoclassicism, with its supposedly "objective" falsifications of "negative truths" which, like every emerging truth obliged to face the "murderous collectivity" (I am paraphrasing Adorno), is in need of laments rather than of neoclassical masquerades. Adorno's dogma involves the whole of musical activity and throws a problematic, but intellectually stimulating, light on the inherent conflictuality of musical creativity, which is an inevitable condition of the work's very existence—conflictuality between the parts and the whole, between appearance and essence, between subject and object, between expression and idea. I call Adorno's view a dogma because it imposes these and other pairs of oppositions (in themselves still meaningful and relevant to contemporary musical creativity) on musical works which are solitary and monumental in their concentration, even when of brief duration (as in the case of Anton Webern). It admits no alternatives to the rending conflicts which inhabit Schoenberg's work and which are capable of raising the expressive tension to the limits of paroxysm. In this perspective, parody is invariably transformed into sarcasm, and conflicts are carried to their ultimate consequences. This dogma seems unable to admit the existence of complementary relationships.

The neoclassicism of Stravinsky and that of Schoenberg are certainly poles apart from each other, but they are also the two very different sides of a musical journey that wants to exorcise and at the same time come to terms with memory and diversities. They are also complementary as, in their different ways, were Wagner and Verdi, Webern and Debussy, Berg and Schoenberg. The seeds of this conflicting relationship with memories and diversities are also present in Mahler. Breaking conventional stylistic codes, he solitarily developed within himself a musical discourse made of contrasting yet complementary forces where, in the same breath, trite melodic signals and compelling ideas, though "institutionally" incompatible with each other, interact. Mahler transcends musical, anecdotal memories in visionary dimensions that had never been heard before: a vision where the specificity and the seductiveness of the motives seem, at times, to talk to the global, problematic symphonic architecture from quite a distance.

Stravinsky's often deprecated neoclassical experience can be seen, obviously, as a selective journey through fragments of history, like a parody, but, occasionally and constructively, also as a form in motion. *Agon*—"Ballet for twelve dancers," written between 1953 and 1957 for George Balanchine—is, in that respect, a fundamental work. It concludes Stravinsky's neoclassical itinerary (if that is what we must call it) in an admirable act of exorcism where the past is approached neither as antiquity nor as an object to be collected, and where each character speaks with the voice of another. It tends to be eclipsed in a musicological "no comment" because, I suppose, it is so difficult to place.

As is the case with any music deserving our interest, all of the constituent elements of *Agon* live a manifold life. Its form pretends to be closed, but only because the final coda takes up the beginning in almost literal terms, while its movement is sporadically marked by symmetrical and minimally varied returns. A describable form can be encountered everywhere: in an improvisation as well as in the shape of the clouds. But *Agon* is above all a container in which Stravinsky has placed a miniature collection of precious objects of various kinds, of different character and provenance, and of great beauty, along with copies of the same objects. Some of them live side by side with their reproductions—they are, in other words, repeated—without, however, suggesting the idea that *Agon* is a commentary on the French *rondeau*. To approach the various episodes, there is no need to refer to a seventeenth-century French ballet manual, although it undoubtedly exerted a powerful influence on Stravinsky's work with Balanchine and, every now and then, also on the expressive character of the individual pieces.

But *Agon* is not a dance suite, not even a parody of it. In *Agon* there's a little bit of everything: diatonic pieces, chromatic, atonal, canonic, tonal, serial, polytonal, neo-Baroque pieces, references to Webern's Concerto op. 24, and also chamber music scattered in a large symphony orchestra that never plays all together. But there are also real developments and proliferations of the material which spill out of the polite formal ceremonials: they spread out, in other words, beyond the perimeters of the individual pieces, placing the symmetries and the repetitions in an ever-new light, and not always a polite one. And then there are self-contained events (like the Sarabande-Step and the Branle Gay) which do not communicate with each other or with the rest—real "happenings," short-lived and gentle. Thus *Agon* proceeds on three different levels: repetition, development, and the insertion of unrelated episodes. But however it may proceed, in its own meta- and hyper-Stravinskyan referential labyrinth, *Agon* is a work characterized by lightness. Lightness, because it communicates at every moment the sensation of having stripped and reduced to the bare essentials of their functions, to pure gesture, to a symbol of their expressivity, some of the frequently cumbersome bodies of the musical legacy.

In the first of the lectures he was to have given in this very place, Italo Calvino wrote: "Most of the time what I did was to take away weight; I tried to take away weight at one time from the human figures, at another from the celestial bodies, at another from cities; and above all, I tried to take away weight from the story's structure and its language." One of the conditions of lightness, I would like to add, is knowing how to withdraw respectfully, without rhetoric, from things, and knowing also how to voluntarily forget them, when the right time comes—"on tiptoe," Calvino would have said of one of his characters who departs headed for who knows where (as he himself sadly did, and all too early).

It is significant that in *Agon,* apart from the passages repeated almost exactly, the intervals are not organized in a symmetrical manner with the "dances" themselves. The same hexachord may be part of two radically different episodes. The same development, the same process of transformation, may involve a succession of different episodes, apparently closed off in themselves, in their own specificity, and rather detached from the process of chromatic transformation. This is the case, for example, of the first three episodes in which the lighthearted opening "fanfare" is contaminated by an innocent minimal chromaticism which, however, gradually spreads over the whole instrumental texture, until it corrupts all the figures and all the motifs of the three different episodes. The process of chromatization is indifferent to the nature and the division of the episodes.

Is this a separation of parameters? No; it is a separation of processes. In *Agon* Stravinsky does not submit himself to history, but he retells it in various different ways. *Agon* is a musical documentary (happily, an untrustworthy one because it is infinitely creative) about historical memory and structural memory and their relationship—itself untrustworthy and transitory. And it is also a farewell to neoclassicism.

Why then forget music? Because there are a thousand ways to forget and to betray *its* history. Because creation always implies a certain level of destruction and infidelity. Because we must become able to call up the memory of that which is useful and then to forget it with a spontaneity that is paradoxically rigorous. Because, in any case, as Heraclitus said, "it is not possible to go into the same river twice." Because the awareness of the past is never passive, and we do not want to be the obliging accomplices of a past that is always with us, that we nourish, and that never ends.

▌ 4 ▌

O ALTER DUFT

"O alter Duft aus Märchenzeit" (O ancient fragrance of times past): this is the first line of the last piece of *Pierrot Lunaire* by Arnold Schoenberg. If I tell you that music, just like life, can also be permeated by old perfumes, it's not to announce that this lecture will be nostalgic or sentimental. Don't be alarmed: the old perfume I will be trying to evoke is that of the "open work," an experience that profoundly marked the musicians of my generation, and which continues, occasionally, to stir up old questions.

There are musical works that are finished, and works deliberately left unfinished; there are works still "in progress," or works involuntarily finished. Or unfinished. Or open-ended. Their finishedness and their open-endedness may manifest themselves in an infinite number of ways, and for an infinite number of reasons. The attempt to draw up an inventory of those reasons is difficult, to say the least, perhaps even contradictory, since one can approach a musical work in many different ways which imply its state of greater or lesser openness and of its being latently in progress. A musical work can never really be "already there" as *Madame Bovary, Les Demoiselles d'Avignon,* the Guggenheim Museum in New York, or *Rashomon* can; these works all describe to us, among many other things, the relationship between their authors' ideas and the criteria for their realization. A musical work is never really *there:* it always needs intermediaries who, through performance, help to clarify and interpret the relationship—always somewhat open—between the idea and its realization. A musical idea that does not carry with itself and within itself the terms of its concrete realization simply does not exist or only exists poorly, or, as we shall see later, becomes something else. A musical work's so-called openness can be found, located, or developed in different places: in the conception of the work, in the performance and the listening to the work, or, and this is the most likely case, in all three places at once.

A conception of musical form that tends toward openness implies the desire—if not exactly the possibility—to follow and develop formal pathways which are alternative, unexpected, non-homogeneous, and most important, not linear. But alternative and unexpected with respect to what? Obviously, mainly with respect to terms established by the composer in the actual conception of the work. In any work that can be defined as open, there is an obvious paradox. In the listening time, though not in the space of the page written by the composer, the result—even with its most complex identity—will always be unambiguous and not open. The page written by the composer will always be the equivalent of a notepad, of a logbook in which different episodes of the creative process are recorded. The performer can wander through the episodes, pass from one to another, ignore some, and invent an order of succession. In doing this, if the musical substance of the ship's log is of great interest, it will enrich the performer's experience, and gratify his or her musical intelligence. It can be argued that the idea of predisposing one material capable of giving rise to multiple forms—in itself intellectually and poetically very attractive—is intrinsic to any creative process, even to one that aims at the construction of a work that ultimately always begins, proceeds, and ends in the same way. The problem is that this kind of formal multiplicity is somewhat aristocratic because it can only be perceived by the composer, by the performer, or by someone who has had the opportunity to listen to two interpretations or versions of the same work in a row.

Reflections upon "open work" and "work in progress" in music have often implied the presence of chance and of random procedures, assumed not only as the true guarantee of the openness of the form, but also as the signals of an ideological repudiation of the very idea of form, and even of the idea of the work itself. Some of you might recall the time when composers, before the random computer programs of the future, used dice to determine pitch, duration, intensity, timbre, and other unpredictable and often amusing parameters. There is certainly no point in regretting what history has not given us, which in any case can only be guessed, but I can't help thinking it might have been better if the repudiation of form and work had also masked a need for analysis and transcendence that obviously could not be obtained by the tossing of dice.

In 1962 Umberto Eco published a book which since has become a classic: *Opera Aperta* (translated into English as *The Open Work*). This book was partially inspired by "open" or relatively open musical experiences such as my flute *Sequenza,* and it develops, within a vast framework, some of the problems I am approaching here. I say problems because such they really are, especially when we avoid a proper distinction between musical and literary concepts.

Without attempting to sum up this important book, let me mention a few points. Eco says: "The form of the work of art gains its aesthetic validity precisely in proportion to the number of different perspectives from which it can be viewed and understood. These give it a wealth of different resonances and echoes without impairing its original essence." He also says that a musical work can be open in a tangible sense, and that it can be concretely unfinished. The author, Eco says, seems to hand to the performer the pieces of a construction kit, being rather unconcerned about their eventual deployment. "This is a loose and paradoxical interpretation of the phenomenon, but the most immediately striking aspect of these musical facts is itself a positive feature: it invites us to consider the need to work in this kind of direction." Eco eloquently explains how this happens, taking the oeuvre of Kafka and of Joyce as the examples *par excellence* of "open" and ambiguous work. He speaks at length about Joyce's *Finnegans Wake* and *Ulysses,* developing Edmund Wilson's famous metaphor of a city animated by a complex and inexhaustible life. He makes meaningful references to Proust, Montale, Mallarmé, Valéry, Dubuffet, Frank Lloyd Wright, and others. In the years following *Opera Aperta,* Eco has no longer pursued this direction, and music has disappeared from the horizons of his search for an "illimited semiosis." Inevitably so, since music—as I suggested in a previous lecture—is not a convenient match for semiology: it seems to challenge its powers.

We are talking about the late fifties and early sixties, when composers were seeking to invent new structural principles that would permit a complete independence from any formal pre-determination. They were hoping to watch new forms emerge in a different manner each time, but always bearing a significant correspondence to the composer's conscience, to his or her instinct and imagination. This, at least on the surface, did not always happen.

With chance—a sort of a well-educated chaos—openness becomes a private affair that concerns essentially the person who tosses the dice, either metaphorically or not, taoistically wondering whether the sound of the rain is or is not preferable to a Beethoven quartet. Composers in those years occasionally allowed chance to choose for them, often with remarkable and hilarious imagination, entrusting chance, or the products of chance, with some sort of aesthetic dimension. But chance introduced music into a different cultural sphere, where the works themselves (as open, virtual, or informal as they may have been) could not undergo any transformation because they simply did not exist anymore; they had disappeared.

It is true that a systematic and fanatically numerical procedure may turn out to be analogous, in its perceptible results, to a random procedure. It is equally undeniable that the awareness of this relative similarity of results is at the root of many significant musical achievements of the last decades. On the other hand, this *coincidentia oppositorum,* this perceptive coincidence of opposites, has been responsible for a number of disasters in both camps; it has become something of an alibi, both conceptually and behaviorally. It led composers—both the obsessively systematic as well as the rigorously random—not to assume all of their perceptive responsibilities: the combinatory processes of the former and the chance operations of the latter generated, each in its own way, a similar statistical distribution of intervals, durations, register, and so forth. This is how, in some cases, any sense of form or structure—as open and complex as you wish—seemed to have vanished, and in order to bring the collapsed structure back to life some brutal formal interventions were needed, leading, more often than not, to incoherence and to the renouncing of something vague that was not really there.

The total serialists invested every note with an elevated number of combinatory functions and determinations that should have quantified and developed, according to identical procedural criteria, schematic musical elements. The result was occasionally expressive (any form of renunciation is somehow expressive on its own), but the project of a formation of musical meaning was reduced to mere functioning: a self-styled microstructure could not be identified, nor could it interact, with a nonexistent macrostructure. Serial procedures were strictly tied to the criteria of non-repetition, yet made a rather cumbersome use of all possible canonic and proto-contrapuntal forms. They were tied to the idea that a form had to die out spontaneously when its combinatorial potentialities had exhausted themselves, yet they were denied, for example, another interesting rhetorical artifice (which we have come across earlier in a different context): that of having a work stop without having it end.

The other group, the "aleatorists" and their near-relatives, the "stochastics," certainly had more freedom of movement in terms of density, dynamics, profiles, and variable tempos. In their indifference to detail and to history, they were exploring, looking at a stopwatch, a sort of macroform, but without the support and comfort of microform. In a case like this, the work may gain in connotation but loses denotation, taking on the overall characteristics of an attractive and relentless natural event. Works of this kind (usually entrusted to an orchestra) could be described as if they were clouds, the wind on the surface of the sea, the clamorous chirping of birds in the forest, or frogs in summer fields—while the author could legitimate them in terms of the calculus of probability, mathematical logic, or the Fibonacci series. Sound-events as metaphor, in other words.

In either situation—that of the generalized series or that of indeterminacy and chance—it is always *detail* that falls by the wayside: the very detail that, more than any other factor, accounts for the completeness, the meaningfulness, and the dignity of a musical work. In the first case the fetishism of the detail, saturated with information, often makes performance and listening almost impractical; in the second case indifference with regard to detail transforms the work itself into one abnormally bloated detail whose result in terms of sound may here and there be rather involving on account of the associations it evokes (clouds, wind, sea, summer fields).

It is nonetheless a fact that this disparity of purposes, criteria, and behavior has served to liberate musical thought from thematic conditioning (from the idea, for example, that the series is a hypertheme of twelve notes); it has helped to open up musical processes to the totality of acoustical processes, to stress the need for complementarity among possible choices and segmentations, and, finally, to make any idea of musical form—however open-ended and temporary it may be—inseparable from the reality of performance but non-tautological.

Is it possible to promote a relationship of reciprocity between systematic procedures on the one hand and random procedures on the other? If such an encounter is to become significant, it must be possible to locate it on a structural platform capable first of all to endow the various behaviors with essentially local functions, distinct from each other but open-ended. They must relate to each other in a way similar to that among harmonic elements and those of tempo and timbre, which can be approached locally, but at the same time they take on and contribute to a more general, global meaning. In a musical construction, local and momentary disorders must be able to interact with equally temporary regularities, synchronies, recurrences, and symmetries—just as, in language, sounds on the one hand and noises on the other, vowels and consonants, periodicity and statistical distribution, interact and interpenetrate with each other. Just as, finally, the idea of open form must be able to compete, not to say alternate, with the idea of closed form. Certainly, they are conflicting experiences, but they are also complementary, for better or for worse they are inseparable, and, more often than might be expected, they may need each other.

The "unfinished" in music is an ambiguous and contradictory dimension. Maybe it doesn't exist. It is contradictory because it conflicts with the desire to complete and, temporarily at least, to conclude a musical work. It is ambiguous because, though it may be the child of chance, though it may dwell within an "open form," it cannot dispense with the experience of "closedness." It is no longer possible to fit the "unfinished" into the utopian aspiration to retrieve that common store of musical knowledge which once brought composer and performer pragmatically together, and which made it possible for Antonio Vivaldi to write that he had not finished the bass line of one of his concertos because, when all was said and done, even a dunce could work it out. Can we get any help from Michelangelo's "unfinished" works, still so meaningful for us today? I think not. Michelangelo was in a titanic hurry, and, once the concept had revealed itself to him, he no longer had the patience to complete the statue in every detail. "You cannot work on one thing with your hands"—he himself wrote—"and another thing with your head, especially when it comes to marble."

In literature, the "unfinished," which is aesthetically and poetically rooted, does not exist, and if it appears to exist, it is often a question of missing pages. The great literary works (Proust, Joyce, Musil, Faulkner, Beckett)—open-ended as far as an amazing number of questions and layers of meaning are concerned—suspend or develop various narrative tempos (themselves open-ended and interwoven one with another), but they are all as finished as cathedrals (as is Robert Musil's monumental "work in progress").

The "unfinished" in music is signaled by notation which may often assume functions analogous to those of a map in preparation for a trip, which is full of implications, of silent details. In one region we may be interested in the waterways, the mountains, the roads, the density of the vegetation, or still other aspects, depending on whether we plan to cross it by boat, on foot, or by car. A map, then, in any case implies choice and a hierarchy of functions, conditions, and representations. Similarly, if we enter an extremely variegated and complex musical territory, it may sometimes be advisable to supply the performers who have to cross it with an incomplete map—that is, with flexible articulatory criteria and with proportional rather than absolute time-relations. The composer may, in other words, allow the performers to adapt the work to their own abilities. Alternatively, if we are entering an extremely diversified and gestural vocal territory, we may perhaps dispense with extremely detailed dynamic and pitch values since this information is already implicit in the contours of the vocal landscape and the gestures that inhabit it. These are cases in which the performer is given local freedom to interpret the text, freedom that may influence certain morphological aspects of the work but not its physiognomy.

The idea of the "unfinished," then, concerns the way

in which the work is represented—its map, the spirit of the work—but not the itinerary, not the territory.

The notion of the unfinished can be taken even further, not so much because more and more extensive yet specific responsibilities may be assigned to the performers and their intuition, but because the map itself (the musical score) may become more and more essential and laconic; it may confine itself to suggesting the envelope of a virtual and vaguely descriptive form, inhabited by long or short presences, long or short silences, rapid interjections or slow afterthoughts, very high or very low notes, *pianissimi* and scarce *fortissimi*. The text thus becomes a renunciation, it becomes impoverished, even spiritualized—it becomes, in other words, the wistful parody of a voyage toward silence.

We hear much talk of silence: of the silence of time in a time of silence, a silence empty and open to the point of pseudomystical delirium; we are told how to be in silence, how to feel and inhabit silence, how to be inhabited by silence. So, silence becomes a mental space, open to everything, also to an impulse toward death. But silence is not an absolute. Musically and acoustically, it does not exist. It can be inhabited by everything and nothing; it is a sort of retinal grayness of musical consciousness. Sounds, even the most conceptualized sounds, are always concrete, they cannot be dematerialized—not even those of Webern, who knew something about inhabited silences.

A musical text, in the mind of its composer, may take the shape of a perfectly closed and conceptually sealed entity. To an interpreter, the same text may on the contrary appear open-ended and fraught with structurally significant alternatives. But a text may also appear open-ended to its composer and closed to its interpreter. Over and above the author's intentions and the listener's *a prioris,* the performer's intentions and *a prioris* also converge in the music. They are the most relevant, but, as we know all too well, the performer is the not always legitimate heir to a terribly complex and burdensome history. In fact, the case is by no means rare of a performer who transforms the relative openness of a work into behavioral freedom, imitating musical behaviors that were once productive of musical sense. But listeners end up having to take what they are offered on faith, not being in a position to ask whether, in the intentions of the composer or the performer, the work was or might have been open-ended, closed, or what have you. Listeners have no choice, because they have no point of reference: everything they hear for the first time is invariably closed as far as they are concerned. They could in fact make a choice, and form an opinion, only if different interpretations of the same text were to be presented alongside one another; or if, in the case of "mobile" works, the order of the components were to be modified; or if the extempore choices made by the performer were to be explicitly signaled—I wouldn't know how—while the audience has a good laugh.

Every form of musical creativity is, by its very nature, open-ended. The fascination of the studies that analyze the creative itineraries of great musical minds (Beethoven, for example) does not lie simply in the account of the creative choices made, but above all in the description of the composer's ability to discover one thing when he was looking for something different. This magnificent ability is fostered by a frequent but momentary detachment between the cells, the details of a musical itinerary, and its overall shape—a kind of brief estrangement between form and thematic material, between macrostructure and microstructure, such as would become substantial in the nineteenth century, in Schubert, Schumann, and especially Mahler. Motifs of great beauty seem at times to enter into a form which receives them with a certain detachment, like somewhat unwelcome and cumbersome visitors. Or doesn't receive them at all. In the Andante of Mahler's Sixth Symphony the hyper-structural E-flat major, as it sounds for the last time, appears like an empty room, no longer inhabited by melody. The melodies have just departed ("sie sind nur ausgegangen").

A different situation presents itself when there are no formal *a prioris*. This is the case with Stravinsky's *Rite of Spring:* the form is substantially episodic and entirely invented—an accumulation of powerfully and autonomously characterized, non-recurring events. The ordering, the "assembling," the editing of part of the episodes was done, so to speak, "on the field," in keeping with a strategy of maximum articulatory contrast and a virtual openness made up of closed forms. You will recall Mahler's torment when he experimented with different possible orders for the movements of his Sixth Symphony. This was not the case with Stravinsky, of course, because—whatever order he might have given to the episodes—the material put to work by him is, for all its diversity and complexity, miraculously homogeneous. And also because he intervenes, connecting *a posteriori* episodes very different among themselves through alliterative procedures that are extremely simple but at the same time display great penetration and great formal astuteness (consider, for instance, the "Introduction" and the "Danses des Adolescentes," or the "Jeu du Rapt" and the "Rondes Printanières"). These alliterations confer added vastness upon the outlines of the *Sacre,* which, as we all know, contains within itself an enormous number of organically interwoven factors, but also levels that are quite indifferent to each other—all of which places the relative autonomy of the individual episodes in a wide-range perspective, dialectical and deterministic at the same time. The *Rite of Spring*, in other words, lives many lives in one. This is its deepest meaning.

From a completely different point of view, this is also a possible meaning of the open work and of open forms—and this is as precise as we can be, because we know that our desire for closure or openness, for order and disorder, cannot necessarily be identified with the actual perception of that openness, of that order or disorder.

Listening to "openness" is always a dilemma. A musical event may present us with extremely complex, chaotic, and diversified sound situations (the musical equivalent of a video-clip commanded by a random program). This will lead us to look for and single out their common aspects, and we will certainly find some, given the already stated fact that, once a point of view has been established, everything can be related by analogy, continuity, and similarity to everything else. At the other extreme, a homogeneous and immobile musical event (the equivalent of a face that never changes its expression) will stimulate us to pick out the slightest differences and variations.

It is obvious that the greater the number and diversity of the elements at play, the greater will be the need (and also the difficulty) to identify the reason for their coexistence—even despite the author's intentions. It is equally obvious that the fewer the number and diversity of the elements, the more specific and discrete will be the details useful for a possible interpretation. We have on the one hand a virtual and indecipherable "macroform," and on the other an easily perceptible and segmentable "microform."

Let us imagine that it is our intention to relate, not by simple superposition, those two distant and mutually indifferent worlds which are governed internally by chance. Let us imagine, on the one hand, reading the macroform with the help of the homogeneous segmentations and details of the microform; and on the other hand, imposing the chaotic and frenetic pace of the video-clip on the microform—that is, on the impassive face. Among the various imaginable outcomes, there is one which promises to be more interesting and more expressive than the others: by means of the exchange of the two temporal dimensions, the two worlds, not in the least similar, meet and join hands, giving musical sense to temporary openings and closings, confirming, if it were necessary, that the musical sense lies above all in the *entente,* in the meeting, even if entrusted to chance, between macro and micro dimensions.

The implications of this perspective are far-reaching, and they bear the scent, the *Duft*, of things new. They relieve chance of its stopwatch, they rob it of its stolid indifference to time diversity, leading music forward into unexplored territories.

In closing, I would however like to suggest that good old, vast, and indefinable open form may have some practical utility, provided it is approached as a pedagogical tool. For example, it can educate children toward purposeful listening; it can give them practice in making choices, in reacting spontaneously, in distributing the bricks and mortar of music, which can be transformed and combined according to different criteria. And this experience brings us an ancient perfume, another *alter Duft*, since "open form" can become a useful substitute for or a complement to the ancient exercises of keyboard bass harmonization, or an extension of certain aspects of jazz improvisation. I am not saying this as a provocation or out of a taste for paradox.

I believe that the experience of "open form," of the "work in progress," of the "unfinished" may only contribute to recovering an ephemeral, lucid, and transitory dimension of musical experience—setting aside all aspiration to an idea of eternity—

and educating us instead to think of the work as an agglomeration of events, without any prearranged center; events which nonetheless find, locally and sometimes surprisingly, their connections, their necessities, and, occasionally, their beauty.

SEEING MUSIC

When someone asked him how he envisaged the stage production of his dramas, Wagner replied that he thought of them
as musical action becoming visible. The profound and revolu-
tionary coherence of Wagner's musical dramas more than justifies this affirmation, by no means as simple as it may seem,
which involves narrative dimensions of a non-visual nature,
endows the visual dimension with an open emblematic function, and implies a certain detachment from the ideals of the
Gesamtkunstwerk. To Mozart the same question would certainly have seemed extravagant, even incomprehensible. But
not to us. Mozart's operas strike us, among other things, as
visualizations of classical thought, of the sonata and concerto
forms. Debussy seems to give visual substance to the ellipses
of his musical thought in an opera, *Pelléas et Mélisande,* which
has no foreplot, which emerges from nothingness and dis-
solves into nothingness, neither eliciting nor resolving moral
conflicts. The succession of the scenes of *Pelléas* seems in fact
to evoke the images contained in "a book of memory," whose
pages are turned, I like to think, while remembering the future.
Alban Berg, with *Wozzeck,* seems to synthesize on the stage the

intensity and rigor of his musical thinking, whose structural complexity is visualized and condensed in a sequence of self-sufficient scenes. The scenic gestures seem like episodes from an imaginary film, skillfully edited by the music.

These examples—and others could of course be cited—serve to remind us how the profound and long-lasting meaning of musical theater seems to achieve complete fulfillment only when the scenic and dramatic conceptions are generated by the musical thought and are structurally analogous with the music, but not necessarily similar. They must be identifiable over a long time perspective, in the overall design, and in the structure of the narrative, while the individual moments may conflict among themselves. The music may express, even describe, the scene; or it may be indifferent to it; it may even conflict with it. The inventions of Kurt Weill and Bertolt Brecht and those of Alban Berg, so different from each other in other respects, are exemplary from this point of view. Equally exemplary was Verdi. In the first act of *Rigoletto*, for instance, we hear a kind of musical jukebox that is completely indifferent to the drama which is taking shape; and then we have the final quartet, significantly and temporarily removed from the drama that is coming to a head; naturally, there are also many descriptions and identifications of emotions and situations.

The transferal of a musical vision onto a stage, and the establishment of a coherent dialogue between musical thought and visible action, is a topic open to all kinds of speculations. There are also countless factors that may disturb or dilate it: moments of spectacular vocal virtuosity, for instance, or technical scenic interferences, which may be more or less meaningful, yet they always carry with them the weight of their history, of their own usage and customs. This dialogue tends to resist theoretical analysis, which can nevertheless be applied separately to each dimension: the music and the dramaturgy, what we listen to and what we see.

Musical time, the time when we listen to music, is mobile and irreversible, while the perception of what stands before our eyes, on the scene, is instantaneously global and selective. In a dialogue between these two modes of perception, it is the perception of the music that conditions the perception of the images: the music permanently analyzes and comments upon what we watch, and not the other way around.

But let us get back to Wagner. During his next to last trip to Italy (he was orchestrating *Parsifal* at the time), he stayed for three months in the countryside near Siena. On a visit to Siena's magnificent cathedral, as soon as he entered, he said: "This is the Grail of Parsifal!" And in fact the stage design for the opening of the Grail in the third act, at the premiere performance of *Parsifal* in Bayreuth, was a fairly accurate reproduction of the cathedral in Siena.

There is nothing unusual about seeing a famous Italian monument on the Wagnerian stage in Bayreuth. Indeed, from Wagner's own point of view, this is perfectly consistent and meaningful, especially when we bear in mind the plethora of citations of historical places, villages, castles, cathedrals, and pyramids that have inhabited the scenes of the operatic stage. But it is also significant that in the setting of *Parsifal,* the cathedral of Siena was in fact optional and was not necessarily used in later performances, just as in practice all of the visual aspects of all operas of all times are optional choices. The music and the text, on the other hand, have their own autonomy and cannot easily be substituted. Nevertheless, what we *see* in an opera, which ought to substantiate and confirm the alliance between words and music, between the meaning of the music and the meaning of the discourse, can also render unstable and even contradictory that alliance: this is what happens frequently nowadays in some re-exhumations of rightfully forgotten operas.

A staging that aspires to something more than mere decoration may contribute to the realization of an opera not so much by providing a specific visual setting for the events and actions, as by suggesting their emotional context, the *Stimmung* of a musical and poetic situation. "We will not try any more to give the illusion of a forest," wrote Adolphe Appia in 1895, speaking of his production of *Siegfried*, "but rather the illusion of a man in the atmosphere of a forest." Appia was the first opera director to criticize radically the traditional "Wagnerian" manner of staging Wagner. He maintained that the Wagnerian stage had not kept pace with the newness of the music, and he was the first to distance himself from scenographic naturalism, doing away with painted scenery altogether: getting rid, in other words, of the Siena cathedral. It is the music, said Appia, that must dictate the conditions of the image. The *mise-en-scène* must present to the spectator only what belongs in the space evoked by the musical text.

What frequently occurred, especially before Wagner, was precisely the opposite. It is common knowledge that the opera genre is historically variable. Over the centuries, it has changed its characteristics and its relationship to the outside world—we have only to think of the radical changes in singing styles, or of how in the seventeenth and eighteenth centuries the operatic stage and its machinery could be authentic experimental models of architectonic research, or projects for works to be carried out far beyond the confines of the theater. The raw materials of opera—lighting, voices, costumes, texts, scenic architecture, instruments—have evolved and been transformed, but, in one way or another, they have carried with them and on them, and continue to carry, the memory and the traces of the uses to which they have been put, uses that in turn led to their transformation and decline.

We have always tended to see the stage as the result of a convergence between a calculated perspective and effect that were in harmony with the accepted moral and civic perspectives, and the intended emotional effect of the operatic narrative. The presence of a story to be told, with words spoken and sung, and the acceptance of theatrical conventions, which tended little by little to be reduced to a matter of mere routine, exerted a powerful influence upon the music and took precedence over it, eventually leading to an already programmed relationship between eye and ear. This conditioning was significant enough to justify a theatrical representation even when the music was essentially made up of mere mannerisms and stereotypes, even when opera made no more sense outside of itself, outside of its pertinacious singing. *Cano ergo sum:* I sing, therefore I am.

We all know that miracles and last-minute surprises, in opera, were perfectly at home. The events narrated always reached their destination. If, for reasons of social class, it was not acceptable for Violetta Valéry to marry Alfredo or for Gilda to leave happily with the Duke, along would come death, that *deus ex machina* which provided a solution to every moral dilemma, however unsolvable, to the tears and satisfaction of everyone present. Still, in the nineteenth century, Italian opera, as much in its most elevated and original moments as in its crudest manifestations, belonged to the people; it was a form of collective ritual, and could therefore become a cultural meeting point providing a sense of collective identity and a facile emotive instrument of social awareness, almost as much as popular songs, marches, hymns, and fireworks.

It remains true even in our own day that any imaginable conception of musical theater or visualization of music (not necessarily Wagnerian) must contend with the countless aspects of a general stage convention, which in turn is made up of a number of specific conventions—narrative and poetic, scenic and musical. It is as if these conventions continue, from time to time, to assert their claims, their right of asylum in the temporal arc of a night at the opera and the proscenium arch of an institutionalized theater. I am not the first to insist that they be dismembered.

Stravinsky was one of the first to propose a prudent but nonetheless significant separation of the component parts of the representation, with a tendency toward a certain disjunction, onstage, between the itinerary of the music and its figurative organization. The narrative planes of the music and its staging display friction and conflicts. Stravinsky himself spoke of musical bigamy—with the scenic gesture on the one hand and the word on the other. The role of the narrator in *Oedipus Rex* or *L'Histoire du Soldat* is, at least in part, to free the characters from the burden of a literal and tautological—in other words, useless—representation of what is being narrated anyway, and to permit them to express a healthy and somewhat cynical indifference. In *Renard* and *Les Noces* the parts mimed onstage and the parts that are sung do not correspond to a single stage presence but are divided between two. And then there is the well-known neoclassical tendency toward "estrangement" between musical invention and musical convention, which allows invention to gain the upper hand over convention at any point and to measure the distance and meaning of that overpowering and the gap that ensues.

Is it still possible today to speak of opera as a genre? Could it be that opera as a genre continues to exist today only because we have opera theaters that feed on it, and because, as Bertolt

Brecht remarked, whatever else happens, the curtain must go up every night—like the morning paper, which must be out on the streets every morning—and the theaters need a supply of material to meet their needs? Could it be, as Brecht suggested, that the so-called worthwhile works are worthwhile only insofar as they are worthwhile in the context of the theatrical apparatus as it exists today? And that if they are worthwhile, this means that they do not pose a threat to that apparatus and that their worth can be measured by a standard based on the notion of marketability? Many years have gone by since these peremptory and somewhat sententious affirmations were made. There can be no doubt that they contributed to a heightened awareness in the handling of the separate ingredients of the operatic production, as well as to sabotaging the psychological accretions of traditional theatrical commodities in general, and to unmasking the dulling effects of so-called high expressive values.

The kind of critical rationalism that Brecht's epic theater imposes on the stage and on the stage/audience relationship, against the idea of illusionistic and consolatory theater, implies the autonomy of the various levels of expression and of all the elements that make up the representation. Music plays a fundamental role, especially when, by reason of its autonomy, it serves to interrupt the development of the action and to alienate it. Text, music, costumes, settings, lights: all have a citational character, and together they produce a performance made up of a series of separate situations and tableaux, leading to an epic dilation of the whole, and creating in the spectator—in Brecht's own words—a tension directed not toward the outcome but toward the development of the action, which, as we know, was meant to be politically instructive.

What Brecht never gave us, however, is an evolutionary view of the means and criteria that govern music theater. His ideological apparatus ("Do not build on the good old days, build on the bad new ones") did not allow him to evaluate the historical fact that, in the meantime, opera and its temples had been transformed into very complicated museums, closed in upon themselves, and cut off from the changing world outside. Theater, with or without music, must preserve the tendency to break out of itself, to speak to a world outside—whether real or ideal—as must be the case with all feelings and ideas, which acquire meaning only when they refer to the reality within which they take shape.

It has been said that a genre is among other things a social convention, and, like all conventions, it produces its own expectations on the part of the addressee, the "theatrical consumer." For this very reason, the opera genre has been subjected in recent years to close scrutiny; it has been completely dismantled, and its component parts, with their burden of memories, have been sorted through, reassembled, discarded, transformed, and, frequently, eliminated. Was this necessary? For me the answer is easy, because that is exactly what I have tried to do myself. Or not to do. Let's see. I would be the first to recognize the countless difficulties one encounters in trying to make music theater on a crumbling stage, a stage which does not allow one to create characters capable of living out their improbable tragedies, a stage, in other words, thronging with the ghosts of opera history.

In *La Vera Storia* (*The True Story*), a musical action in two parts, I was partially and ideally close to Brecht, but also to Italo Calvino, the author of the text. Ours was an ambitious project. We wanted to approach the essence of opera theater in its prime elements, and we also wanted to suggest that a "true story" is always different from the way it appears at first sight and that in back of it there may be another story that is even truer.

As in a folktale, the first part of *La Vera Storia* presents the main outlines of an elementary plot, within the conceptual frame of the feast as sacrifice, of carnival as a parody of sacrifice (a theme developed by Mikhail Bakhtin). It does not go deeply into psychological conflicts, but transfers them into a musical paradigm capable of encompassing other conflicts and other details. There is a general air of indifference with regard to the characters—who are not really characters—but a great deal of attention, on the other hand, is given to the narrative functions they explicate. In fact, the non-characters in the first part of *La Vera Storia* could wear another story and could be placed somewhere else. The narrative is treated like an object which changes and in its turn modifies its subject.

The acoustical and visual oppositions of what we usually call "teatro all'italiana" imply a well-tested agreement among all its elements. For us, all of those elements have already been theatricalized to start with. They are "operatic," they already "sing," they have already had opera experience. Indeed, they are the product of that experience. This is why it may be difficult to take that agreement for granted, and it may be more useful, in a Brechtian manner, to separate the elements of the performance in such a way that a harmony and an alliance can be rediscovered on a new footing, in the same way that by discovering new connections we give meaning and value to music while we listen to it. That same way allows us to travel from opera to music theater. To do this, we must invent an open time relationship between what we see and what we hear, in a space that must be discovered, since it is part of a process and not an *a priori*—an open space but not an empty space. A prearranged coincidence and unanimity and an uncritical synchronization between musical, scenic, and textual connections tend to downgrade the discourse.

As I said earlier, in the first part of *La Vera Storia,* as in a folktale or an opera, the participants are identified according to their roles and their vocal specificities. Tenor-ness, soprano-ness, and popular-narrator-ness are treated like pseudo-characters. As such, however, they are not prisoners of a libretto: it must be clear that they are there by chance and that they could get out at any moment. And in fact in the second part they have all gone away. But Calvino's text has remained—it hasn't gone away, it is still there, more or less the same as it was in the first part. It has simply been cast differently. The second part becomes a transfiguration and an analysis of the first, in an entirely different musical and dramaturgical perspective. The two parts develop the same text in different ways—as if a narrator were to propose two different versions of the same event. But while the first part tends to display the images and the shapes of a folktale, the second part does not seem to narrate a thing. It "thinks" about the first part. In the first part there are vocal protagonists, in the second part there is a vocal collectivity. The first part is concrete, the second part is dreamed. The first part does not ignore the operatic stage; the second part rejects it. The first part is "horizontal," bright, outdoors, *en plein air;* the second part is "vertical," wintry, set in the city, nocturnal. The second part is an obscure parody of the first.

This transferal and re-reading of the same text in a different space and time certainly has its roots in popular narration, but it also responds to a need to forget and to make up for an absence: the absence of a story. Lyric opera, especially when it was not dealing with divinities and the marvelous but with real men and women, had a tendency to take place in the present, to the point that when a foreplot had to be narrated, things often became twisted if not ridiculous. But opera had melodies, motives, melodic and orchestral formulas which developed a dramaturgy of their own, parallel to the events taking place onstage. These unforgettable motives were marked, from their first appearance, by a very visible and tight relationship with specific characters and situations onstage.

Without all this, where does the true story of *La Vera Storia* lie? In the first or in the second part? I don't know. Someone watching and listening might well come up with the hypothesis of a third part, truer than the other two perhaps, and maybe similar to those invisible cities and gardens of Calvino, whose terraces overlook "only the lake of our mind."

From this point of view, *La Vera Storia* deliberately intends to raise a number of questions, but I prefer to think that the only answers possible are the experience of the theater itself—a bit like questions about music which, when you get right down to it, only music itself can really answer. Leaving the experience responsibly open, it is my hope that the musical theater can continue to be, also today, a terrace overlooking the world. Is this a utopia? Then long live utopia! It is a privilege to be protected, especially when we are searching for something we are not sure of finding, when we are searching for things that do not yet exist because they do not have a name. And perhaps never will.

At this point, the "expectations" of "theatrical consumers" may no longer be worthy of our interest. If we wish to engage in a dialogue with them, we must frustrate them and, above all, we must attempt to educate them to separate and analyze the different elements of the work. We must create favorable—but not necessarily pacific—conditions so that by means of analysis the musical performance can assimilate the setting and the words, and be totally assimilated itself into the stage performance. The whole becomes one.

A continual shifting of our attention from listening to watching and back again to listening can act as a provocation and put constructively to the test those notorious and much-maligned "expectations." For their part, the "theatrical consumers" will have no respite, precisely because, all too often, consumers are all they are, and only with difficulty can they perhaps be persuaded to appreciate the advantages of a listening eye or a seeing ear—an eye that listens to a host of different things from the same point of view, and an ear that sees a single thing in different lights and from different points of view.

Outside and away from opera, a musical performance may become a nonspecific form of theater. Watching the actions, gestures, efforts, and acrobatics of musicians who are doing unusual, chaotic, even comical things, no doubt serves to assist and to round out our listening. It is certainly interesting to see how unusual and attractive sounds are produced, particularly if these sounds are part of a coherent musical organism which has generated them. There is no reason for alarm if strictly musical organizational criteria, which organize sound in time, are transferred also to behaviors outside of music, but visible and concrete—in time. The distant roots of this possibility of transferal can be found in popular traditions, in the often unexpected relationship, for example, between music and work in the fields. Dance too, with its rigorous choreographic criteria, can be seen as a sublimated expression of the same relationship.

The need to coordinate the various modes and timings of visibility of strictly functional musical behaviors with non-musical behaviors has been encouraged in part by past experiences of electronic music—heard through lonely loudspeakers—and by the need it created to make up in some way for the absence of visual referents. Performers interacting with prerecorded sounds—or sounds produced and controlled by a machine—and the spatialization of sound are examples of conventional ways, certainly open to new developments, of inhabiting and performing space, of stimulating a dialogue between what we hear and what we see, or could see or would like to see, given the fact that whenever we listen to any intentionally musical sound we have the irrepressible tendency to look for connections with some human action.

There are instrumental or vocal theater experiences which may find their center and expressive coherence in two alternative directions—in operations, that is, that I would like to define as either additive or subtractive. In the first case, each participant is involved in an exorbitant number of musical functions and relationships which, organically added all together, find their justification and refuge in gesture, in a sort of "stage word"—*parola scenica*—of listening. In the second case, the musical work is tampered with, reduced to a few performance details which, isolated in this way, tend to acquire an autonomy on their own (breathing in different ways but without producing sounds, for example)—a situation which is in danger of falling prey to the anecdote, to facile parody and to kitsch.

I have myself experimented with the first case, that of performers saddled with more work than they can handle, in other words, with an excessive number of musical functions. I was interested at that time in exploring the possibilities of a listening experience devoid of a prearranged dramaturgy rooted *a priori* in the musical structure, but instead a dramaturgy deduced from and generated by the musical process.

This was the case, for instance, with my own first steps, in 1961 and 1962, in the territory of musical theater, which I had not yet explored but for which I had been refining the instruments—once again like a memory of the future—especially through Monteverdi's *Orfeo*, his *Combattimento di Tancredi e Clorinda*, the Eighth Book of his *Madrigals*, and the implications—more than the actual realizations—of the *Madrigali rappresentativi*, the "theater for the ear" of the Late Renaissance. I am thinking of my already mentioned *Circles*, based on three poems by e. e. cummings, for female voice, harp, and two percussionists; or *Visage,* for the same female voice—that of Cathy Berberian—and electronically produced sounds; or *Passaggio,* for soprano, orchestra, and two choruses, one onstage with the orchestra and the other spread out among the audience. Let me say a brief word about *Circles,* which was performed at Tanglewood in 1960 with Cathy Berberian and the soloists of the Boston Symphony Orchestra.

The exorbitant number of musical functions and relations in *Circles* can briefly be described as follows. The three poems by e. e. cummings, of increasing complexity, are repeated twice: I, II, III and III, II, I, in an ensemble of five episodes. Poem number I is taken up again at the end with musical elements of the second episode. Poem number II is taken up with elements of the first episode, while poem number III, in the third episode, repeats itself backwards. The harp reproduces and expands upon the modes of attack of the voice and the percussion instruments; e. e. cummings's text, interpreted by the voice, is then developed musically and extended acoustically by harp and percussion. The three cummings poems take on the role of generators of musical and/or acoustical functions. There is a continual oscillation between periodic figures, bounded by specific constellations of intervals, and complex gestural events characterized by a notable degree of indeterminacy. The choice and use of the percussion instruments and of the harp are dictated by specific phonetic models: the instruments play, so to speak, the voice and the words. They play different modes of attack, vowels and consonants (fricatives, sibilants, plosives, and so on). The instruments translate and prolong the vocal behaviors, insisting upon them, in a sort of onomatopoeia or, rather, vocal-instrumental bilingualism. The relationship between a female voice and two frequently unrestrained percussion players can present problems of balance. The singer must therefore move around, following an itinerary which will allow her, in succession, to be accompanied by the instruments, to be like them, and, in the end, to be completely absorbed by them. This very intense dialogue between the musical dimension, the phonetic-acoustical dimension, and the spatial dimension is maintained and developed through a particular coordination assigned to musical signals and mainly to the gestures of the singer's hands; she seems to be celebrating a rite of total identification with the other performers. These signals are assimilated to the musical process, making *Circles* a theater of over-abundant relationships. The score itself becomes a multilayered protagonist that is evoked, realized, and translated in visible and diversified musical behaviors.

I would like to mention, incidentally, that the criteria of notation are themselves a way of seeing and thinking music. Without the development of notation in the Middle Ages, music would never have become an encoding of the world; the problem of devising criteria for the quantitative description of an empirical and qualitative experience would never have arisen; there would have been no polyphony (as we understand it in Western culture); there would never have been and there would not be musical experimentation or ongoing research, nor, I suppose, a notion of the uniqueness and originality of the musical work itself.

Instrumental or vocal theater may find its center in operations of a subtractive nature. Any single detail, isolated and decontextualized, becomes something else and may acquire autonomous and different functions. What went previously unnoticed (the breathing of the musician, for instance), and was taken for granted as part of a coherent overall behavior, is now foregrounded and tends to become significant in and of itself. Since it does not completely lose contact with the overall behavior of which it is a part, it becomes a parody. If one eliminates all the consonants in a discourse, emphasizing maybe the inflections and the intonations, the vowels, left by themselves, become something else, and produce a "little theater" of paradoxical and humorous effects. Parody again!

However, if only because of its etymology and its ancient history, parody is not always the amusing and minor form of disguise and often comic escape from reality which invades theatrical forms. Instrumental theater sometimes presents us with a quite serious, even tragic, form of parody. This is true, for example, of the instrumental and vocal metatheater of Mauricio Kagel and his extremely serious, talmudic parodies. His "dissection of what existed—has been suggested—does not reveal the truth, it reveals nothingness." Often, what one sees while listening to his meta-music is something like the tragically pessimistic ghost of Samuel Beckett's *The Unnamable*.

Music theater, seen from that point of view, is not always explicit and it does not necessarily produce action but, rather, thought. In practice it tends to be self-referential. When its experience expands beyond the boards of the stage, this does not occur by means of an illusory psychological extension of the stage space, but by means of our processes of thought. Instead of miracles, it offers fascinating and ongoing research.

The impulse to seek a union between image and sound comes to us from very far back, and is rooted in an ancient synesthetic vision of the world. Let me recall Exodus 20:18: "And

all the people saw the voices...and the sound of the shofar."
The link between light and sound, between light and word, is
common to all narratives of origins, of primordial events, of
myths and apprehensions of the world; and music often appears to be the most powerful mediator between the eye and
the ear, between the mobile and extreme points of a space that
has still to be explored and interrogated. A space that seems at
times to lead us to the threshold of a mystery. A space which—
with stage sets, lighting, costumes, voices, and instruments—
we insistently endeavor to secularize, but which despite all our
efforts always seems to contain an intangible, perhaps a sacred,
core.

▌6▐

POETICS OF ANALYSIS

In this lecture I would like to present a few ideas on the various ways in which poetics and analysis may coexist—ideas which imply the ambitious and maybe unfulfillable desire to develop a relationship of interdependency, of complementarity, if not of identity, between the creative and the analytic levels of music.

We are all aware—because we have been reminded of it time and time again—that any discourse on music is by its very nature condemned to be partial and incomplete. So partial indeed, and so incomplete, that in this final lecture I find myself in the position of making statements which could probably be refuted by an alternative discourse which maintained the exact opposite! I do so, not out of homage to the notion of open-mindedness (the mind is in any case open), or of a "work in progress" of the spirit, and not even as an homage to dialectics—aimed, that is, at developing ideas through contradictions—but out of an inner need. This time I will be talking about things that are implicitly bound up—more closely than has usually been the case until now—with my own work, trusting that it is free from an excess of contradictions.

The two terms—poetics and analysis—could perhaps be lumped together in a single definition—"music criticism"—by analogy with "literary criticism" or "art criticism." But I must confess that I have some trouble with such a formulation, because it would force me to assume—and this might prove difficult—apparently objective attitudes, which could only partially turn out to be musically useful. In fact, to use the synthetic and tactful expression "music criticism" would amount to the same thing as saying "analysis of poetics"—which is almost the exact opposite of what I want to talk to you about here.

To begin with, I would like to submit for your consideration a somewhat oversimplified and perhaps pretextual idea of poetics and musical analysis—the first of course being an extremely ancient term, while the latter is a relatively young one. Today, the notion of a musical poetics is no longer a subject for discussion and has no need of adjectives. A first name and a last name are generally sufficient. We can talk, in fact, without fear of being misunderstood, about the poetics of Anton Webern, of Olivier Messiaen, of Igor Stravinsky, or of Béla Bartók, thereby implying a diversified and consciously original vision of the making of music. It would, on the other hand, strike people as somewhat strange if we were to talk about the poetics of Bach, Haydn, or Mozart, since their works, for all their complexity, tend to incorporate objective historical and aesthetic values which, at the time those works were composed, had an existence of their own, quite independent of the individual works themselves—values, in other words, whose relative permanence was not easily altered by history and events. The notion of poetics, however general the term, has always implied self-awareness, and an evolutionary view of music-making and of the criteria that guide it. Whenever description enters into the specific details of a given work, poetics gives way to analysis.

Two thousand years ago, the idea of analysis could have been considered something akin to "logic," derived from the so-called theoretical sciences (such as physics and mathematics). This reflection may produce nostalgia and forbidden desires in some modern neo-Aristotelians, but the fact is that today most musical analysts seem to need all the adjectives they can find—maybe too many. Thus we have formal analysis, semiological analysis, structural analysis, harmonic analysis, hermeneutic analysis, rhythmic analysis, neo-positivist analysis, phenomenological analysis, qualitative and quantitative analysis, statistical analysis, melodic and stylistic analysis...you name it! If, on the other hand, the analyst is a composer, there will be no need to choose and specify the categories and criteria he or she intends to adopt because, whatever the circumstances, the analysis will always be self-analysis: composers will not be able to help projecting themselves, their own poetics, into the analysis of the work. The composer reveals himself on the couch of someone else's work. Even in cases of the greatest generosity and aloofness (Schumann's analysis, for instance, of Berlioz's *Symphonie Fantastique*) or of extreme far-sightedness and objectivity (Pierre Boulez's analyses of Wagner, Debussy, and Berg) the chief analytical instrument at the composer's disposal will always and in any case be his own poetics. Indeed, it is fortunate for us that this should be so (enemies that we are of the hypothetical—and soporific—notion of musical objectivity), and fortunate too for anyone who believes as I do—I've said it once and I'll say it again—that, when everything is said and done, the most meaningful analysis of a symphony is another symphony.

Common sense would seem to suggest that poetics and analysis are synonyms, and completely overlap with one another: that the poetics of Stravinsky, for instance, finds confirmation in, and is to be identified with, the harmonic, rhythmic, and metrical analysis of *The Rite of Spring*, while a structural analysis of *Les Noces* will confirm another phase in Stravinsky's evolution. But a composer's poetics is always something different from its analyzable aspects—like a form, which is always something more and different than the sum of its parts.

A text is always a plurality of texts. Great works invariably subsume an incalculable number of other texts, not always identifiable on the surface—a multitude of sources, quotations, and more or less hidden precursors that have been assimilated, not always on a conscious level, by the author himself. This plurality constantly imposes fresh points of view on the analysis. An analysis which is committed to describing the most minute details and the microstructure of a work—considered deterministically as a function of its overall form and macrostructure—is only possible provided that the alliance between the two dimensions is immanent and their interconnection can be taken for granted perceptually (as it is, for example, in the analysis of a classical form). There are works characterized by extreme concentration and at the same time by extreme diversification. This is the case with Stravinsky's *Rite of Spring* or *Jeux* by Debussy: they are works where a tendency toward autonomy of character and structural relations, on the one hand, coexist with independent, deductive, and generative processes, on the other. Harmonic, timbric, metric, and rhythmic matrices, on the one hand, coexist with evolving thematic cells, on the other; complex and discontinuous articulations coexist with repetitive and immobile events. In works such as these, or other works of comparable complexity, the only analysis possible is a sectorial analysis—an analysis, that is, which reflects the tendency of the listener to perceive the various strata in a segmented way. But to choose a possible segmentation of the musical process and to tailor the analysis to the specific characteristics of the work under scrutiny does not necessarily mean building a bridge toward general theories, toward a universal grammar of analysis. If this were the case, so much the better if the analyst is also a composer: there would be a better likelihood that his analysis would have something to teach us about *his* poetics, about the specific and concrete production of the compositional process, the manifold ways of existing of their component elements and their segmentation.

Like all experiences which tend to produce value judgments, any form of analysis, if it is to play a musically significant role, must be capable of being reflected in a historical perspective—if for no other reason than that compositional techniques and the practice and instruments of music are historical variables.

We frequently find today that, even in the case of the most penetrating and, so to speak, scientific analyses, the analyst is not very concerned to place the work under examination in the context of the composer's chronological development—in the context, in other words, of his or her poetics. It is precisely this tendency toward atemporality that makes musical analysis an open and creative experience which, however, may become pointless when the analyst is struggling with the conceptualization of something that does not exist.

Analytical creativity is in danger of becoming aestheticized when, with procedural elegance, it pursues a relationship of identity between the form and the meaning of the analysis. In order to perform an analysis of the meaning of a work, the analyst finds himself obliged to guarantee at all times that the analysis is meaningful, not merely as an instrument but, as is more frequently the case, as a theoretic configuration. Consequently, his poetic vision and the analytical procedures he applies will be inevitably determined by the criteria of the analysis itself, which frequently have little or nothing to do with the poetics of the composer examined. The analyst who applies to the work a previously elaborated theory—compatible above all with itself—becomes a parody of the composer who has the sacrosanct need to be able to construct a sound architecture compatible with the structural criteria of the composition itself. In fact, we can think of analysts who, in the course of their investigations, seem to evince an ill-concealed feeling of antagonism with regard to the composer—with regard, that is, to someone who analyzes music by making it. Their creative impulse thus takes on a negative turn: rather than search for the meaning of a work, they use the work to clarify the meaning of their own analytical procedures. The analysis then becomes a guarantee of the analyst's objectivity and of the non-biased nature of his or her instruments, and the work enters an analytical enclosure, like a Trojan horse.

Analysis, as I was saying, implies creativity and may develop as an independent activity, indifferent to the composer's intentions and to the work itself (clear manifestation of those intentions), which is treated as organic matter predisposed by some biological divinity. In such a case the analyst resembles a fisherman who, knowing what he wants to catch, throws his specially made net into the sea and catches only what fits the net that he himself has woven. There is one name we can't avoid mentioning in this context—that of Heinrich Schenker. His vision of the musical experience is preordered like a natural phenomenon. He casts his three-layer net and fishes out a boneless Beethoven deprived of any metrical or rhythmic component, reducing the thematic dimension to a symbolic phantom; but he is reluctant to venture into the troubled and ever-changing waters where a Debussy lurks, or a Stravinsky, or a Webern—all Schenker's contemporaries—or, alas, even a Wagner!

There are cases in which analysis is brought to bear on experiences which do not easily lend themselves to linear and numerical description. In such cases the creativity of the analyst may experience some difficult moments, especially when dealing with something that has no immediate meaning (a sound doodle or an accidental and indecipherable noise) but which can be made to mean something. Even within the frame of the most self-referential analytical strategies, a constructive and adventurous flexibility in the relationship between what the analyst wishes to demonstrate, and what is analyzable but not demonstrable, can be developed.

Analysis, like music itself, makes sense when it confirms and celebrates an ongoing dialogue between the ear and the mind. This is why I have always felt some detachment from the old dodecaphonic analyses which sought out the twelve notes in the various forms of the series in all their possible combinatorial operations, forgetting that, while the notes may be the screws that help hold the wood together, they are not the table. I nurture the same feeling of suspicion for the theories whose main concern seems to be building shelters against the incursions of the diversified, noisy concreteness of the world as it is, in the process of becoming, or as we would like it to become. Metaphors apart, we are talking about shelters which preclude a dialogue between the substance of sound and the substance of music, between the ice of rigor and the heat that lies below it, between the sound of sense and the sense of sound. At their worst, such theories take the form of authoritarian systems—intolerant and dogmatic—which, in their own little way, preach the elimination of the outsider. The poetics of analysis thus becomes the politics of analysis—a search for procedural pedigrees. It is at this point that the history of music comes in and hands over the check, which the analysts, predictably—especially if they are a bit of a Schenkerian or a neo-positivist—find themselves unable to pay.

At times the composer-analyst may give in to the temptation to provide an apparently objective—that is, mathematical—statement of what he is up to. This is perfectly understandable, since, in difficult moments, there is safety in numbers. Everything in this universe can be reduced to mathematical models. What a mathematical model and a musical work have in common is the reduction of a vast field of possibilities to a *unicum,* whether it be an algorithm or a musical text. The difference, however, is the following: we cannot reconstruct, on the basis of an algorithm, the vast field of possibilities which generated it. It has no memory of where it came from; it is deaf and dumb. Whereas a musical text—which proposes a pact, not always peaceful, between senses and intellect—bears with it and upon it the traces of the trajectories that formed it, of the roads taken, of a host of previous texts.

The sense of emptiness that is transmitted by certain analytical systems and criteria that are particularly difficult to assimilate comes from the vast inhabited space, from a "no-man's-land" that lies between the analysis of the organization of the notes and the musical substance (between the notes, that is, and the sound), and between the analysis itself and the theoretical speculation that seems to promote the idea of an imperturbable and essentially passive musical form. I wish that ideal of absolute form (a new kind of *musica mundana*) and that no-man's-land could open up and communicate through concrete and creative trajectories: through a true poetics (or *poiesis*) of analysis. The ultimate sense of these trajectories can be revealed in the traces of those already covered and of those yet to be covered. It is our duty to keep tracing and retracing new paths: in the words of an old Spanish saying, there are no roads if nobody is walking.

Musical experience seems at times to want to go beyond listening, and in such cases, as I have already said, it gets translated into words. Today we can find examples of complete estrangement between the practical and sensory dimension and the conceptual one, between the work listened to and the process that generated it. The more pronounced this detachment is from the experience of listening, the more intrusive is the presence of critical discourses which claim to explain how this or that piece by Bartók or Beethoven, or Webern or Wagner works—as if these composers themselves had transcended the experience of listening. Such commentaries make the work appear "Hamletic," not so much because it becomes incomprehensible, but because, like Hamlet, it is reduced to "words" and "loses the name of action." As the epigraph to *Real Presences*, George Steiner quotes Georges Braque's dictum "Les épreuves fatiguent la vérité" (proofs tire truth), while, in quite another context, Wittgenstein has claimed that "what we cannot speak about, we must pass over in silence." I would like to propose a paraphrase which seems suited to the present instance: the truth we cannot speak about, we must sing, we must say it in music.

In the past, semiology seduced us. With their urge to catalogue everything and their breathless search for an unlimited semiosis, semiologists often seem to be on the run. But music is not in a hurry: music's time is the time of the trees, of the forests, of the sea, and of the large cities. Musical semiology was an attempt to go beyond the dualism implicit in musical procedures and to lessen the distance between music and analysis. In the first lecture I alluded to the kind of musical semiology that derived from linguistics, in the 1970s, and that was significantly commented upon by Nicolas Ruwet and David Osmond-Smith.

Successively, there have been other attempts which were more attentive to the functional strata of music. One, in particular, drew my attention but raised in me irresolvable doubts. In order to give an account of music's "symbolic specificity," Jean-Jacques Nattiez developed a semiotic model that "takes account of its triple mode of existence—as an arbitrary isolated object, as a produced object, and as a perceived object." Thus the musical text *in itself* is to be seen as something separate from the musical text as the product of the composer's intention, and from a perceived text which takes shape in the ears and mind of the listener. I feel that it is a question, here, of a somewhat unrealistic division of responsibilities. The intentions of the composer are a rather abstract and often contradictory compound to explore. We can insist on the fact that the sketches of Beethoven or Schubert are fascinating because they throw light on their creative process. But semiology can cope only with the notion of a fully realized work, when the intentions of the composer have been, in one way or another, already fulfilled and are made available for a constant and diversified questioning that escapes an "intention" versus "result" binary relation. In that triple semiological perspective even the listener becomes an abstraction. Partially removed from any concrete context, he or she is required to embody the quintessence of all possible textual interpretations, to approach a global awareness of all possible musical experiences. Finally, the "neutral level"—the "produced object," namely the score—tends to reduce the musical text to something immaterial.

I don't see how musical experience can be contained, today, within this kind of tripartite vision. Given the rather diversified, heterogeneous, and glossolalic world in which we operate, we should try to provide, with our own work—that is, with our heuristic instruments—the possibility of analyzing and assimilating diversities. Otherwise we might just as well return, indeed, to Boethius and take refuge in the sumptuously ascetic Greco-medieval theory of music which confirms the idea, to quote Umberto Eco, that "the more the system explains experience, the more it prescinds it."

It was Saint Augustine who said that in order to find truth, man must not only look inside of himself but he must go beyond himself. And it was, again, Severinus Boethius who, with his idea of musical knowledge, gave his seal of approval to the accessory character of sensible perception with respect to truth.

A number of composers, in a more secular intellectual context, of course, have been known to declare that they have no interest whatsoever in the technical problems of the performance of their music, and that they are not even interested in knowing what it sounds like. What interests them is how it should be written. Professionally and socially speaking, this is certainly a daring position. It is above all a new one, since at least fourteen centuries have gone by since the theory and practice of music became technically, anthropologically, and psychologically inseparable. It may also be an interesting position, since this distance between thought and matter presupposes an idea of music as a instrument of knowledge instead of an instrument of pleasure. Knowledge of what? What kind of pleasure? The colors of Matisse, Pollock, and Rothko can be analyzed with a light-frequency meter, and the perfume worn by an attractive woman is subject to chemical analysis. In good weather and bad, the moon and the stars are variously observed by poets, farmers, businessmen on holiday, and astrophysicists. Perceptual space can be analyzed on the basis of concrete acoustical and musical experience, or with the instruments of neurophysiology.

Once again, we are faced with an empty space. We could attempt to cross it and to fill it with meaning, if it were not bounded by an algorithm on the one hand and unperformable clouds of sounds on the other, by algebraic speculations on one side and tautological tintinnabulations on the other.

Does this represent a flight from colors and perfumes, the moon and the stars? And from musical reality—granted that we can define it without having recourse to rhetorical figures? Of course it does. Not even the parascientific language of so-called musical conceptualization can give that empty space a meaning, because, however minimally, it has itself had a hand in creating it—with its stubborn insistence on considering sound processes independently of the way they are perceived, or on separating, in a formalistic way, the so-called "parameters" of music (pitch, dynamics, timbre, and time, that is, the morphology of sound), things that our perceptive abilities are not capable of separating. If it is impossible to make a phenomenological distinction between sound and noise, how can we ever hope to separate, for instance, pitch from timbre or timbre from dynamics? Neo-positivist analyses make frequent appeals to science, but it is significant that they seem to dismiss the science of acoustics (I am not talking about Helmholtz's acoustics, which explored musical sound as a stationary and periodical—and therefore as an abstract—phenomenon, however correct it may be mathematically, but about the recent research conducted at the Bell Laboratories, at Stanford University, or at IRCAM on the diffuse instability and the developmental nature of every aspect of every significant sound phenomenon).

Analysis is not just a form of speculative pleasure or a theoretical instrument for the conceptualization of music; when it contributes to a topology of the coming into being and the transformations of sound forms (and not only by means of the new digital technologies), it can make a profound and concrete contribution to the creative process.

The composer can give every pertinent musical element a double or a triple life. Or a multitude of lives. He can develop a polyphony of different sound behaviors. History of music, from this point of view, is a teacher of developmental processes. We call (or we once called) a succession of different pitches a "melody," a "theme," a "motif," a "row," or a "subject." Each of these terms has enjoyed, as we all know, a variety of complex vicissitudes. Their expressive identity, and the presence or relative absence in them of structuring factors, are in the hands of the composer; but they are at the same time the result of those same vicissitudes, made up of theoretical orientations, subjectivity, techniques, and of expressive, evocative, and even descriptive codes. A melody, an identifiable series of pitches, is therefore the meeting point for a number of functions of a primary nature (harmony, relative dynamics, timbre, rhythm, and meter) or a secondary nature (for example, a vocal or instrumental melody). A melody always carries with it the trace of these functions, or of part of them: it evokes them in a more or less explicit way, or it contradicts them. Polyphony was built and held together on the melody of the *cantus firmus* or of the tenor. A symphony was constructed on its themes and on the harmonic relations which they signaled and embodied. Arias, lieder, canzoni, and cabalettas were made out of tunes. Fugues were guided by subjects and counter-subjects. The implications of what I am saying are obvious and far-reaching at the same time. But the point I want to make—in a nutshell—is that the theme or motif, overloaded with investments and structural experiences and expressive codes, has become transformed into something new. It has mutated. It has become hyperthematic.

If previously, as late as Brahms, the theme was generated and conditioned by specific harmonic, rhythmic, and metrical functions, it now becomes itself the generator of analogous functions, and of others besides. It becomes a generative nucleus, a cell made up of a few elements, a regulator of musical processes. The theme in itself has disappeared; it has become fragmented, hidden, though it pervades all the textures, coloring them with its colors: it is everywhere and nowhere at the same time. But the process is not irreversible. Led on by the generating nucleus, we can retrace our steps and make possible the emergence of a new theme, a new figure—surprising perhaps, different, even alien, but nonetheless generated by those nuclei, by those textures, and destined to transform itself in its turn, to be absorbed and to disappear once again. The timings of this continuous process of transformation and substitution, of this alternation of birth and disappearance of the figures which remain inscribed on our memories in all their specificity, help to create the varying degrees of fusion of the whole and a greater or lesser identifiability of the figures.

At this point we could talk about the harmonic and acoustic space in which these figures, themes, and nuclei succeed each other, but this is not the right occasion for doing so. I have been speaking to you, instead, of possible forms—not of demonstrative but of operative forms, in other words, of processes, or formations. Not forms of development but forms which *are,* which gaze within themselves as they come into being. Not passing forms but forms which *remain,* which observe themselves in their continual internal self-renewal. Forms which stir and question memory but at the same time deny it. Silent forms which tend to make us forget the processes that generated them and which hide the vast number of "vanishing points" that inhabit them. Forms, finally, which live in harmony with analysis and its poetic reasons.

And having said this, I must regretfully bid you adieu. I am grateful for these one-sided encounters of ours, because they have led me to formulate thoughts (and themes) that might otherwise have remained concealed in the folds of my music.